# Hold My Hand

All About the Blessings of Volunteering

Judy Bornstein
2017

Printed in the United States of America

First printing 2017

ISBN-13:978-1976477461

Judy Bornstein
Website: *www.judybornstein.wordpress.com*
Email: *judybornstein@outlook.com*
Facebook: Search for "Author Judy Bornstein"

Cover photo used with permission by The Times Media Co., who holds
the copyright.

For Rudelle —


who gave me the opportunity
to share my compassion with
those who are dying—while
discovering the birth of my own
needy soul through the blessing of
volunteering.

# Table of Contents

Chapter  1 - Michael ................................................  1

Chapter  2 - Faith .....................................................  5

Chapter  3 - Madeline .............................................  9

Chapter  4 - Eileen ................................................  13

Chapter  5 - Adam ................................................  17

Chapter  6 - Irene ..................................................  21

Chapter  7 - Susan ................................................  23

Chapter  8 - Bruce ................................................  33

Chapter  9 - Beverly .............................................  35

Chapter 10 - Kathleen ..........................................  39

Chapter 11 - Arthur ..............................................  41

Chapter 12 - Mabel ..............................................  45

Chapter 13 - George .............................................  47

Chapter 14 - Beth .................................................  51

Chapter 15 - Emma ..............................................  53

Chapter 16 - Bert ..................................................  59

Chapter 17 - Greta ................................................  61

Chapter 18 - Marilyn ............................................  65

Chapter 19 - Danny ..............................................  71

Chapter 20 - Joe ...................................................  73

Chapter 21 - Ruby ................................................  79

Chapter 22 - Thomas ............................................  83

Chapter 23 - Dominic ...........................................  87

Chapter 24 - Abigail .............................................  89

Chapter 25 - Lillian ..............................................  91

Chapter 26 - Elise .................................................  93

Chapter 27 - Jean .................................................  95

Chapter 28 - Henry ...............................................  97

Chapter 29 - Alice ...............................................  101

Chapter 30 - Agatha ...........................................  103

Chapter 31 - Benjamin .......................................  107

Chapter 32 - Bertha ...........................................  109

Chapter 33 - Joseph ...........................................  111

Chapter 34 - Stanley ..........................................  115

Chapter 35 - Barbara ..........................................  117

Chapter 36 - Art .................................................  121

Epilogue .............................................................  123

# Song and Hymn Index

| Name of Hymn | Author | Year | Chapter |
|---|---|---|---|
| Abide with Me | Henry F. Lyte | 1847 | 15 |
| Amazing Grace | John Newton | 1779 | Introduction |
| Away in a Manger | James R. Murray | 1841 | 7 |
| Be Still, My Soul | Katherine von Schlegal | 1752 | 26 |
| Blessed Assurance | Fanny Crosby | 1873 | 4 |
| Breathe on Me, Breath of God | Edwin Hatch | 1878 | 35 |
| Danny Boy | Frederic Weatherly | 1910 | 19 |
| For the Beauty of the Earth | Follist S. Pierpoint | 1864 | 30 |
| In the Garden | C. Austin Miles | 1913 | 2, 20, 24 |
| Jesus Loves Me | Anna B. Warner | 1860 | 7 |
| Just as I Am, Without One Plea | Charlotte Elliott | 1835 | 15, 20 |
| Let Me Call You Sweetheart | Beth Whitson | 1910 | 6 |
| Near to the Heart of God | Cleland B. McAffee | 1903 | 27 |
| Old Rugged Cross | George Bennard | 1913 | 3, 8 |
| Praise to the Lord, the Almighty | Joachim Neander | 1680 | 17 |
| Softly and Tenderly Jesus is Calling | Will L. Thompson | 1880 | 15 |
| The Touch of His Hand on Mine | Jessie Brown Pounds | 1913 | 12 |
| Turn Your Eyes Upon Jesus | Helen L. Lemmel | 1922 | 11, 23 |
| What a Friend We Have in Jesus | Joseph M. Scriven | 1855 | 21, 28, 80 |
| When I Survey the Wondrous Cross | Isaac Watts | 1707 | 5 |
| When We All Get to Heaven | Eliza E. Hewitt | 1898 | 25 |

# Forward

*In a culture not inclined to confront matters of death and dying, it is indeed rare to find someone who considers being fully in the presence of both as privilege and gift. Judy Bornstein is just such a person, and her stories serve to remind us of the inseparable connection between acknowledging our mortality and discovering transcendence.*

Donald J. Evans
Elder Law Attorney

*When I met Judy Bornstein and learned of her singing ministry to the sick, the lonely, and the dying, I told her, "You are a musicianary; aka a musical missionary." Within these pages the reader will find the love of the Risen Christ pouring over the patients Judy visits.*

*"I was sick and you looked after me...Truly I tell you, whatever you did for one of the least of these brothers and sisters of mine, you did for me."*
*(Matt. 25:36b, 40)*

Rev. Esta Rosario
United Methodist Pastor of the Indiana Conference

*True vignettes shared by a friend and "co-worker", a hospice volunteer. Music, especially hymns, is the common thread that opens doors and binds the author to her patients at this critical time of life.* Hold My Hand *is a collection of non-denominational stories that will appeal to all.*

Laura Harting
Retired Executive Director of Visiting Nurse Association

Hold my Hand *will take you to new levels with the high rewards of volunteering. Judy's experiences, as she vividly explains, will encourage you to look beyond the moment.*

Sandi Pettit
Retired long term care nurse

# Preface

This book has been arranged so that each chapter is a true story. Each person's name has been changed to protect their privacy.

This book was written in the spirit of deepest gratitude...
for the purpose of sharing
love for one another in its purest form.
JB

If the only person who reads these words
and sees my heart therein is Jesus,
then my humble satisfaction is complete;
because He will then see the depth of my thankfulness
for leading me down the path that He wanted me to travel.
JB

*"Because of His kindness, you have been saved through trusting Christ. And even trusting is not of yourselves; it, too, is a gift from God...It is God himself who has made us what we are and given us new lives from Christ Jesus; and long ago, He planned that we should spend these lives in helping others."*
Ephesians 2:8, 10 (TLB)

# Acknowledgments

I am deeply humbled by and indebted to:

    -- The many hospice patients and their families, my friends, and my neighbors who welcomed me to share the challenges and blessings of their journey through the Gates of Heaven.

    -- Don Evans, friend and legal advisor, who saw something of value in me that I never saw in myself.

    -- Laura Harting, whose vision and dedication established the Visiting Nurse Association/Hospice of Porter County NWI, which gave me the opportunity to discover the deep fulfillment of volunteering.

    -- Rudelle Crowley, Hospice Volunteer Coordinator, who trained me, encouraged me with her praise, and shared with me the amazement of how often God led me to be in the right place at the right time in order to share in the beautiful, peaceful transition from life on earth into eternal life in Heaven.

    -- My thanks also to the four VNA staff/volunteers who edited my book; Maria Galka and Joyce Hicks. Also Lizz Frenzel, who went above and beyond just editing, as she patiently worked her magic on the computer. Finally to Sandi Pettit, who intertwined her editing into a very lovely friendship.

    -- Tom Oakwood, for his expertise in photography as he generously formatted my drawing to fit into this book.

    -- Pam Gonzalez, who graciously, patiently, and expertly took my manuscript and handled every detail of getting it published.

Note:
A portion of any profits from the sale of this book will be given to
VNA/Hospice of Porter County, NWI.

# Introduction

## HOW SWEET HE IS

The story of how I began this absolutely overwhelming chapter of my life journey, which is called volunteering, was a bigger surprise to me than to anyone.

When I woke up early on a snowy, dreary winter morning, I had absolutely no idea that I was going to retire. As a matter of fact, the word retirement was not even on my radar. I was extremely entrenched in the rut called "my life."

I remember reading about the pioneers who traveled west in the primitive days of the settlers long ago. One particular passage had always stuck in my memory. As a wise old man had bade farewell to a young family about to embark on that long, lonely journey, with all their worldly goods in the buggy being pulled by their team of horses, they were advised of the treacherous roads they would encounter. The old man said, "Be aware of the rut you will travel because you will journey in it for a long, long time."

After living a lonely childhood followed by five decades of two manipulative, abusive, even lonelier marriages, and surviving a devastating hurricane at the age of 68, I started my life all over again as I had begun it. Alone.

But free. Free to reconnect with my children and my family from whom I had been estranged. Free to have friends and communicate with strangers on the street or in the store. Free to worship, to enter a church, to sing out loud. Free to express my ideas. Free to drive again. Free to talk on the phone privately instead of always using the speaker phone so conversations could be controlled. Free to invite someone to come into my home to eat or to talk.

It took four years to shed the cloak of brainwashing and control to realize that I was/am a survivor. Having become suddenly single so late in life, I slowly started to build my confidence in myself by starting life over, for the third time, both financially and emotionally. I began my new life having no relationships with other people except my "far away" family and a couple of distant friends and acquaintances. Gradually I found the gift of neighbors becoming friends.

I had my job in telephone sales where I worked from my home office fourteen hours a day, six days a week, something I had done for the same company for the past thirty years. Actually I had done every type of telephone work, interspersed with a couple of other jobs for fifty-one years. With the exception of a few years, at the insistence of my husband, all my work life was spent in the solitude of my home office, never socializing with co-workers. I surely knew all about discipline and the work ethic.

As I began to rebuild my life, I was totally responsible for repairing my damaged condo. Following the four hurricanes which had wreaked havoc in the span of four weeks in the summer of 2004, I started over. When the eye of Hurricane Charley roared overhead with winds of 171 miles per hour, it felt as if my life was being sucked out of me. It was. My old life was leaving with the wind. Twenty minutes later, in the total and absolute absence of any sound, being surrounded by overwhelming, breath-taking silence, I was aware that my soul had not been damaged. With no money, no car, and no experience at making decisions, large or small, I learned all about the "one step at a time" way of life.

Two years after the life-altering assault to that beautiful, peaceful little town in Florida, I moved back to my roots in northwest Indiana. My husband of thirty-two years had left six weeks after the storm. In the rebuilding process, I felt like a butterfly emerging from a cocoon as I slowly repaired my self-esteem as well as my condo. Two more years went by before the world of volunteering entered my life.

At that point, I had spent seventy-two years living in a mode of survival of one kind or another. One month after I moved back to northwest Indiana, I went to my lawyer to change all my official papers from the state of Florida to be in accordance with my new home in Indiana. After I signed the last of the many papers necessary to bring everything up to date, my attorney, whom I had met at church, quickly became my friend. He worked the sound booth and would smile at me on those Sunday mornings when I had begun to sing solos, in witness to my blessed new life, free to worship and sing after decades of keeping my Jesus secretly in my heart, hanging on to His love, His companionship, and His protection in absolute total silence.

As he was putting all the various legal forms he had created into a large brown manila envelope, Don asked me, "Well, Judy, what are you going to do with the rest of your life?"

I smiled and said, "My goodness, nobody has asked me what I wanted to do 'when I grew up' since I was seven years old." He was sitting there and waiting for my answer. I looked off in space and said, "Well, if I could do anything at all, with no thought to anything else, I would sing. And I would live a regular life with regular people."

He grabbed the clean brown envelope which held all those official papers and scribbled a name and place on it. Then he said, "I have a client in the nursing home who played the organ in her church for several decades. She has no family, only a nephew in California. I try to visit her once or twice a week, but sometimes my case load doesn't leave me enough hours in the day. Will you go and visit with her and sing to her? Just tell the nurses that you are my advocate." He made it sound so simple.

I don't remember if I even answered him, because how did we get from his asking me my dream for the rest of my life to my going to see a stranger in a nursing home? The only time I had ever been in a nursing home was when my mother was dying. She'd had a massive stroke and lay comatose in a facility over a thousand miles from where I lived at the time. I flew to see her the day before she died. She was non-verbal so we had no conversation. I remember sitting beside her, holding her hand and just talking to her as if she could hear me. There wasn't a lot to say because she had never raised me. From the day I came home from the hospital at the time of my birth, I lived with my widowed grandmother. My mother was not maternal.

The next morning, I looked at Don's scribblings on that otherwise clean legal envelope. I made a few calls to customers, as was my habit as soon as I was finished with my breakfast, my devotions, and my one-mile morning walk. I kept staring at that envelope and thinking how kind he had been to me, to guide me through the legal process, giving me confidence that my affairs were in order. I was not particularly anxious to go see this ninety-two year old woman whom I didn't even know. But, on the other hand, if I didn't go, what would I say to him when I saw him in church the next time? After all, he had cared enough about me to ask me to share a dream with him, a dream that I had not even formulated in my mind at that point.

So, only to satisfy my lawyer/friend, I looked in the phone book for the address of the nursing home where his client had been a resident for a long time. I was glad when I saw it was in a town about eighteen miles from my home, because that would "let me off the hook." Since I had not driven a car for thirty-two years, except on very few occasions, I was not confident driving anywhere outside of my newly adopted home town, especially in the snow to a town that I had never seen before.

Like other things that had been a part of my sad second marriage, my husband manipulated my comings and goings because we had one car and it was his. The keys were his. He drove me everywhere, truly everywhere, because that way his control was absolute outside the confines of our home, as well as inside.

So for another hour on that wintry, January morning, I made more calls to more customers and tried to forget what had been asked of me. But I couldn't get rid of the nagging in my brain that kept reminding me of Don's kindness to me, to pay attention to the "real me" who had been hidden from people for so many decades.

Once again, I looked in the phone book, and decided I needed to have a better excuse for not driving to the next town. So I dialed the number listed and when the receptionist answered, I said, "I know this will be the strangest call you'll have all day, but does your facility allow just anyone to come in and sing in a patient's room?" Of course, she put me on hold. Then another woman answered, to whom I asked the same question. She asked me the name of the patient, and then she asked my name. I added that I was asked by my attorney to be his advocate to visit with her and sing to her.

To my surprise, the woman on the other end of the line answered very quickly, "Oh that would be lovely. When can you come?"

I stammered and said, "Well, I live in Valparaiso, and I am not familiar with your facility."

She said, "It won't take you half an hour to get here," and she proceeded to give explicit directions. She thanked me for calling and that was the end of our conversation.

So, after the most cautious driving ever, I finally pulled into the parking lot about an hour after my phone call to the woman in the nursing home. When I entered the front door, I know I probably looked lost, not just because of my unfamiliarity with a care facility, but also because I didn't know who to ask to find that patient.

When a nurse came up to me as I was just standing inside the front door (undoubtedly looking very bewildered), she said, "Are you the woman who sings?" What were the odds? She said, "I will take you to see Mary." And with that we hustled down one hallway, then turned a corner, and yet another until we entered the room where I saw a very small patient who seemed to melt into the bedding. The nurse went up to Mary's bedside and, in order to wake her up gently, she kissed her on the forehead. She said, "Hello, sweetie, there is someone here to sing to you." And with that, she turned to me and said, "Enjoy your visit." and walked out of the room.

Oh, my! What was I supposed to do? What was I supposed to say? Why had I put myself in this position? Why was I there? I realized Mary was looking at me in a slight manner of disgust at being wakened, only to be faced by a stranger. Quickly, I told her my name and told her we had a mutual friend in common, mentioning Don's name and his request to stop in and see her in his absence. That relaxed her...and me. Then I showed her my hymnal and told her that I loved to sing the familiar hymns, adding that Don had asked me to share some of them with her. I asked her if it would be alright with her, and she nodded, as she had tubes attached to both arms, oxygen tubes in her nose, and another tube in her mouth.

So I simply opened the hymnal and sang a couple of songs.

She seemed to enjoy listening to them and even smiled a couple of times. Then I started to sing, "Amazing Grace." When I had sung only "Amazing Grace, how sweet the sound that saved a wre..."

"NO," she said in a voice so gruff that it startled me. So I stopped singing immediately.

I said, "Oh, I'm sorry, I will sing something else," thinking she didn't like the choice of hymns.

Then she mustered every bit of energy she had and said in an unsteady voice, "How sweet He is."

I could see that talking was a huge effort but what she said was very important to her. As she looked right at me, I stood by her bedside trying to think what she meant, when it occurred to me what message she was trying to give me.

"Oh, do you mean..." and I started to sing again..."Amazing Grace, how sweet *He is* to save a wretch like me...."

She smiled a weak, but lovely smile that I had, indeed, understood what she said and, more importantly, what she had meant.

So, once again, I started that beautiful old hymn, only that time I sang it "her" way:

*"Amazing Grace, how sweet HE IS*
*To save a wretch like me.*
*I once was lost, but now am found,*
*Was blind, but now I see."*

She listened to these words and nodded with a peaceful contentment. I was almost overwhelmed with the powerful message I found in the simplicity of changing those two words, from "how sweet the sound" to "how sweet He is."

In that split second, I felt the changing of those two words and the changing of the meaning to be directed right at me! Because of my background of living an overwhelmingly, suffocatingly, lonely life, even as I shared a house with a husband, I found new meaning in the "amazing grace" of His saving me from losing my mind in just trying to survive all those many previous years. I knew firsthand that living in loneliness is totally different than living alone. I truly "once was lost, but was now found, was blind but now I see."

I went on to sing a few more hymns, but seemed to be in a kind of fog as years and years of thoughts were racing through my mind to this particular place as I stood in the room of a woman I had never seen before, who was clearly at the end of her life. And, unbeknown to me at that time, I was at the beginning of the new journey of living my brand new life completely surrounded in peace.

As I was leaving, I took her hand and thanked her for sharing those powerful four words with me. She smiled at me, very grateful that I had understood. *Really* understood. I asked her if I could come back and see her again and she used what little energy she had to squeeze my hand. She closed her eyes and I felt the peacefulness that had filled that room after such an awkward first few minutes together.

Little did either of us know that those were to be the last words she ever spoke. She died that night.

I walked out of her room and didn't know if I should turn left or right in the hall in order to find the outside door through which I had entered. I had completely forgotten the "route" through the maze of halls which I had walked in this strange building filled with more inner doors than I had ever seen. Doors which led into rooms filled with an assortment of people in various stages of physical need.

After many wrong turns I finally saw the door which led to the spot where my car was parked. However, I was totally unaware that you don't just open an outside door and walk out of certain nursing homes. As I pushed the door, the loudest alarm screamed all around me. I turned and faced the long hall I had just walked and said, to no one in particular, "I did that. I did that," as if confession for my loud "sin" would not alter my future freedom! When an aide came up and pushed some numbers on a pad next to the door, the screaming stopped as abruptly as it had started. She looked at my shock at the unexpected noise, and I think, for an instant, she thought they might be needing to tend to me as a patient!

I swiftly walked out to "freedom", only to find that a new dusting of snow had fallen while I was in there, covering a thin layer of ice beneath. Not only did I have to concentrate mightily on reversing my route in this unknown territory in order to find my way home, but I also had to maneuver my car on slippery roads, something I had not done for decades.

Looking back on that short but challenging trip there and back, I realize "How sweet He was" to have kept me both calm and safe. And the challenge of that was highlighted by the brief experience with Mary, as she witnessed to His goodness in her last breath. My gratitude at pulling into my garage was very real.

But the emotions and experiences of that morning had been just the beginning of the emotions and experiences for the rest of the day. And also for the next chapter in my journey as I began a brand new adventure on a never-before traveled path of my life.

Mary's life was ending. Mine was just beginning. I was about to make some monumental decisions. And I was filled with such an overwhelming feeling of peace that warmed and melted any hint of the icy fear of doubt, or the potential storm of the unknown.

My mostly solitary lifetime was about to end.

The simple lunch of hot soup took me a long time to eat as I sat in total silence. Having no idea what was ahead of me, I took the first step to my new life as a volunteer. After rinsing out the bowl, I sat down at my desk, picked up the phone, called my supervisor, and simply retired.

*Then Jesus said to the disciples,*
*'If anyone wants to be a follower of mine,*
*let him deny himself and take up his cross and follow Me.*
*For anyone who keeps his life for himself shall lose it;*
*and anyone who loses his life for My sake shall find it again.'*
-- Matthew 16:24, 25

A big part of volunteering is listening to God's voice –
going where He wants you to go
and
doing what He wants you to do.
-- JB

# Hold My Hand

All About the Blessings of Volunteering

Judy Bornstein
2017

*Preach the Gospel all the time. If necessary, use words.*
--St. Francis of Assisi

# Chapter One

## *Michael*

Understandably, I was a little apprehensive when I went to the bedside of my very first patient, a very ill man named Michael. He was 49 years old. His sallow skin, sad eyes, and rotting teeth confirmed the fact that he had no known address. My files showed that he had no family. He had no history, no friends...nobody.

On my first visit with him, what little conversation we had was very awkward. So I smiled and said I would be back again to see how he was doing. Thinking that maybe he wasn't having a good day on our first encounter, I went to see him again the next day.

He seemed surprised to see that I did come back.

As I was standing by his bed, I asked him if he ever saw any birds at the feeder just on the other side of the window in his room at the nursing home. He turned down the TV and smiled very slightly and nodded. Then he said, "Every day, when I went to the same park bench to feed the squirrels, I had two blue jays who came right up and ate out of my hand."

I got all excited and said, "Oh, Michael, I have never, ever heard of a blue jay eating out of someone's hand. I'm sure they must have thought of you as a friend when you fed them so often." So we found something to talk about.

With each visit, however, I noticed he was growing considerably weaker. His room was silent now and his eyes were closed most of the time. One day I asked him if I could sing "Amazing Grace." He nodded that it would be all right. When I finished, he said very weakly, "That's my favorite."

I had never seen anyone in his room. He truly didn't belong to anyone. His whispered answers had now just become a slight nod of his head.

One day when I went to visit him, I said, "I know what your favorite hymn is. Is it all right with you if I sing you one of my favorite hymns?" He nodded very slightly.

*Precious Lord, take my hand, Lead me on, help me stand.*
*I am tired, I am weak, I am worn.*
*Through the storm, through the night, lead me on to your light.*
*Take my hand, Precious Lord, lead me home.*

*When my way grows drear, Precious Lord, linger near*
*When my life is almost gone.*
*Hear my cry, hear my call, hold my hand lest I fall.*
*Take my hand, Precious Lord, take me home.*

His eyes were closed and he was very still as I had softly sung that beautiful hymn. I stood there and let the Lord continue to speak through me and said, "Michael, you know the squirrels and blue jays are waiting for you in Heaven, don't you?" He nodded weakly.

I asked him if he was ready to take the Lord's hand and walk that path toward the Gates of Heaven and feed them again, and I saw the slightest smile on his face. After a couple of minutes of silence, I bent over and kissed his forehead and told him that I loved him. Within a whisper of time, he died.

Shortly after I got home, the phone rang and it was my volunteer coordinator. She knew he had been my first patient, and the nursing home had called her to tell her that he had just died. She knew that my very own daughter, also aged 49, had died just a few months before of the same condition. She asked me if I was all right. I, of course, had been overwhelmed by that experience, and told her what had happened in his room. We both wept at the beauty of it all—that I was able to be with him and that he wasn't alone. Then I asked her, "When will his funeral be?"

And she replied, "You just gave it to him."

I then asked her when his obituary would be in the paper so I could cut it out and put it in my hymnal, marking that particular hymn that had taken on a very special meaning to me. She said, "There will be no obituary because nobody knew he lived, so nobody would know he died."

I had visited him nine times in the thirteen days I had known him, and yet he will be in my heart forever. He gave me a gift. He let me into his life.

*And if, as my disciple, you give even a cup of cold water*
*to a little child, you will surely be rewarded.*
-- Matthew 10:42

*Guide me, Lord, to notice the hurting, sick, and lost.*
*Help me as I help them, regardless of the cost.*
-- Author unknown

*Lord, speak to me that I may speak*
*in living echoes of thy tone;*
*As thou has sought, so let me seek*
*thine erring children lost and lone.*

*O strengthen me, that while I stand*
*firm on the rock, and strong in thee,*
*I may stretch out a loving hand*
*to those upon a troubled sea.*

*O Use me, Lord, use even me,*
*just as thou wilt, and when, and where,*
*Until thy blessed face I see,*
*thy rest, thy joy, thy glory share.*
-- Frances R. Havergal, 1872

# Chapter Two

## *Faith*

I had been particularly fond of Faith, a dear white-haired lady whose blue eyes and sweet smile reminded me of my grandmother. She had been listed as "failure to thrive" and had been getting noticeably weaker each time I had visited her. When I first began to call on her, I discovered she loved to sing the old hymns. She would smile at every note and every word from those familiar hymns she had sung most of her 95 years because many memories were running through her mind whenever she heard them.

One day, when I went to her bedside, she opened her eyes when I touched her arm. She smiled that lovely smile and said right away, "Dear, I am too tired to hold my eyes open any more, so will you go ahead and sing. I will just listen this time." She was quite hard of hearing, so I bent closer to her so she could hear me.

After singing several hymns that I knew she loved, I then sang her favorite, "In The Garden." She smiled weakly as she listened. As I was finishing up the second verse, I noticed a nurse standing in her doorway, motioning for me to come out in the hall.

I finished that chorus and said, "You seem tired this afternoon. Would you like to take a nap and I'll come back tomorrow?"

She smiled and said, "Yes, dear, I'll wait for you to come back."

I left Faith's bedside and the nurse pointed to the room just across the hall. The door was about half-way closed. She said, "The patient in there just died two minutes ago. She and her two daughters were listening to you sing. When I told the family that their mother had just taken her last breath, they said, "In The Garden" was their mom's most favorite hymn. Would you ask that lady to please come in here?"

When I entered, the two daughters were weeping as they stood by the bed, one on each side of their mom, who lay there looking so peaceful. We had not said a word, but I went and hugged each daughter individually. They then asked me if I would please sing "In The Garden" once again.

So I stood at the foot of the bed and sang that song which had such special meaning to all of them. Knowing that it was the last thing their loving mother had heard on earth, they said they wanted it to be the first thing she would hear in Heaven.

I then asked one of the daughters if she had a favorite hymn, and she said, "That was mine, too."

The other daughter said, "Do you know 'Precious Lord, Take My Hand?' That's my favorite."

I asked each of them to take one of their mom's hands, and I reached for their other hands as we formed a circle around the bed. As I sang those meaningful words, "Precious Lord, take my hand, lead me Home," you could truly feel the presence of Jesus in that darkened room—and see the Light of His presence. Through their tears, two daughters and a total stranger shared in the glory of ushering one of His children into the Kingdom of Heaven.

I left that room as quietly as I entered, never knowing their names, nor they mine. But for those few minutes, we were all a part of the Family of God, sharing in the glory at the end of a life on earth and the beginning of a new life in Heaven.

*As occasion and opportunity open up to us, let us do good to all people.*
-- Galatians 6:10

*Thank you for the privilege we have*
*to serve you by serving others, Lord.*
*-- JB*

## In the Garden

*I come to the garden alone*
*while the dew is still on the roses,*
*And the voice I hear falling on my ear,*
*the Son of God discloses*

*He speaks, and the sound of his voice*
*is so sweet the birds hush their singing,*
*And the melody that he gave to me*
*within my heart is ringing.*

*I'd stay in the garden with him*
*though the night around me be falling,*
*But he bids me go; through the voice of woe,*
*his voice to me is calling.*

Chorus:
*And he walks with me, and he talks with me,*
*And he tells me I am his own;*
*And the joy we share as we tarry there,*
*None other has ever known.*
-- C Austin Miles, 1913

HOLD MY HAND

# Chapter Three

## *Madeline*

After a church meeting one evening, a quiet, efficient, and dedicated member came up to me and asked if I would do him a favor.

He went on to tell me that his mother had recently been admitted to one of our nursing homes, and wondered if I would call on her when I went around seeing my patients. I told him I would be happy to and would look in on her the next day.

He said, "She is 96 and somewhat confused. Since my father died many years ago, and I am her only child, my wife and I try to go to see her every day. But it would be nice if she had someone else to call on her, too. And, by the way, she is an atheist."

I smiled and said, "Howard, as long as she speaks English, we'll be fine."

He also added, "She can be somewhat…well, not nice." I assured him that she was just a friend that I haven't had the pleasure of meeting yet, and I would go see her the next day.

When I went in, she was…yes, kind of…well, not nice. I introduced myself, and quickly added, "I am a friend of Howard and Margaret. We work together at the church."

I always carry my hymnal with me on every call. She quickly looked at that book I was carrying, and she snapped, "Is that a Bible?"

I said with a smile, "No, it's my hymnal."

She then shot back at me, "Are you a minister?"

I smiled again and said, "Nope, I am just a lady who loves to sing old songs, old hymns, patriotic songs, just any song."

She then said, "Well, you can sit down if you want to." So I did. She was sitting in her recliner beside the window in her room and I commented on how bright the sun was that mid-winter day.

I said, "It makes me think of the song 'You Are My Sunshine,'" which I then started to sing. When I got to the second line of that old song, she simply started singing along with me. We smiled and sang it all the way through.

Not wanting to press my luck, I talked about how I had seen my daffodil leaves just poking up out of the ground the other day, and I had already seen the tips of my crocus leaves the previous week, not remembering that I had ever seen them up that early in the year before. So we talked about flower gardens of long ago. I told her I didn't want to tire her out and would come back in a few days. She warmly invited me to do so.

It was a dark, cold and dreary day outside when I returned again not long after our first visit. She remembered me and said, "Please sit down dear," as soon as she saw me enter her room.

We talked about how we ever did the family laundry "way back when" in those Januaries of long, long ago. How we had to heat the water to fill the old wringer washer and then carry the clothes outside to dry. And how the diapers would be frozen solid from the time we pulled them out of the clothes basket sitting on the snow-covered ground and hung them on the line. We wandered down memory lane and ended up being so grateful we live in America and have been able to see the advancement of life through the generations. I then asked her if she would help me sing another song, and getting really bold sang, "God Bless America." She sang most of it with me!

Then she asked me to sing something else. So, I opened my hymnal to see if that would irritate her. No reaction. So just at random I started to sing, "The Old Rugged Cross." Imagine my amazement, when she joined me! She knew most of the words. I did not want to act like I was surprised, so I went back to talking about the olden days.

She interrupted me a few minutes later and said, "Would you please sing 'The Old Rugged Cross?' That is my favorite."

Oh my! I realized in her dementia she had not remembered what had happened five minutes ago, so I sang it again...as she, too, sang along. Since I didn't want to overstay my welcome, I said I needed to go before the weather got too bad. And, again, she asked me to come back.

She began to spiral downward very quickly after that. Of course, I had told her son about the amazing visits we had had on both of our previous visits. He was so grateful. When I saw him in church the next Sunday, I asked him how he thought she was doing, and he said, "I think she's failing fast." The following week she was taken to the hospital, and was soon put in the loving care of the staff at the Hospice Center.

The next time I saw Howard and his wife, he said she had been in so much pain, but almost immediately after entering Hospice, she was much less agitated. I stopped by to see her on my way home from church that morning.

She was lying there very quietly. Even though there was no response from her, I began to sing "Abide With Me," "Softly and Tenderly Jesus Is Calling," "Be Still My Soul," and her favorite, "The Old Rugged Cross." As I left, I told her I would see her again sometime, somewhere, and we would continue our good visits together.

She died very peacefully that evening.

How blessed I was to be able to give her only child a last gift from his mother—the knowledge that even though she told him all along that she was an atheist—he learned as she was leaving this world that she found comfort in her long-held secret that his God was real to her too.

*I was sick, and you visited me.*
-- Matthew 25:36

*Help me the slow of heart to move*
*by some clear winning word of love;*
*Teach me the wayward feet to stay,*
*and guide them in their homeward way.*
-- Washington Gladden, 1879

## THE OLD RUGGED CROSS

*On a hill far away stood an old rugged cross,*
*The emblem of suff'ring and shame;*
*And I love that old cross where the Dearest and Best*
*For a world of lost sinners was slain.*

Refrain:
*So I'll cherish the old rugged cross,*
*Till my trophies at last I lay down;*
*I will cling to the old rugged cross,*
*And exchange it someday for a crown.*
-- George Bennard, 1913

# Chapter Four

## *Eileen*

The first time I met Eileen was on a sunny day as she was sitting in her wheelchair in the dining area of the Alzheimer's unit in a local nursing home.

As a Hospice volunteer, I had been asked to sing to that group of residents living behind locked doors, which granted them the care that gave them safety in the silence of their remaining days, weeks, or years.

When I entered the room, Eileen smiled a beautiful smile which lit up her eyes and her face. When I started to sing, she reached out her hand for me to hold. We were instant friends, although I never heard her speak in the several years I visited her. She communicated to me with her smile.

But I knew that she loved music. And even when her voice was taken from her, she still "sang." For the first couple years of our friendship, she would begin to move her hand when I started to sing, as if she was directing the music. And when I sang, she whistled. Her eyes danced and she whistled. When the directing and the whistling stopped as the years progressed, the smile continued. Oh, she made me feel so special when, in the last months, I would waken her to let her know I was there, and even out of a deep sleep, she would focus, and then smile that special Eileen smile of hers.

Even in her forced silence, Eileen still expressed her faith and her love of life. When she whistled along with me as I sang, I thought of the Scripture passage in the tenth chapter of Zechariah, which tells of lost sheep who have no shepherd to protect them. And then in the eighth verse the Lord says he will hear the cries of his sheep and says, "When I whistle to them, they'll come running, for I have brought them back again." Sheep don't understand words, but they know the sound that signals the shepherd's presence.

At the end of Eileen's remarkably accomplished life, she didn't always understand the words, but she whistled because she always knew her Shepherd was near.

The power of Alzheimer's did not rob her from continuing to witness to her faith in her Lord. It did not diminish the power of her witness through the steadfast love of her devoted husband and loving daughters. One day when I walked into her room, as her last days were numbered, I heard a tape recording being played in the silence of that room. One of her daughters greeted me with a hug and then told me the tape was a speech that Eileen's mother had given, and the family wanted Eileen to hear her own mother's voice again, since they would be meeting in Heaven soon.

I'm sorry I didn't know Eileen in her vibrant years. But she taught me so much in her silent years. We had an unusual friendship in that all of our communication was in singing and whistling and smiling. Whenever I think of her, which is often, I still see her smiling.

Alzheimer's patients are lost in His love. . .

-- JB

"Perfect submission, all is at rest;
I in my Savior am happy and blest,
Watching and waiting, looking above,
Filled with his goodness, lost in His love."
-- Fanny J. Crosby, "Blessed Assurance"


To love someone
is to know the song in their heart
and
to sing it to them
when they have forgotten the words.
-- Unknown

# Chapter Five

## *Adam*

It was mid-morning on Good Friday.

As had been my custom for the past five years, I was making my rounds to sing and visit with the residents and patients in several nursing homes. I began by singing in a couple of dining rooms while they ate their breakfasts, stopping in the rooms of several patients. I also shared hugs and simple songs with the lost souls behind locked doors in the Alzheimer's Unit.

Included in my rounds was visiting in the physical therapy rooms at a couple of facilities, where I often times found a different group of patients each week who were being encouraged by therapists to do their exercises. The staff likes the break in the routine because they can observe the patients in a different way since the residents tend to sing along with me. When they sing, they are continuing their repetitious exercises. Their minds are on the music and the words, and not on the reason they are in the room. This is especially evident if the therapist is attempting to move an arm or a leg in a different direction, possibly causing a bit more pain.

As I began my visit, together we sang a couple of songs, including some old hymns in keeping with the solemnity at the beginning of this Easter weekend. When I asked if any of them had a favorite, a sweet lady said, "How Great Thou Art." I remarked what an appropriate song that was for this particular day.

The room contained mostly women on this visit. However, I had noticed a man sitting in his wheelchair with his back to me. I realized that his lower limbs were moving up and down methodically. And then it became obvious that the machine was moving his legs; it was not the legs moving the machine.

So I began to sing the beautiful requested hymn and there were a couple of women who sang along as they repeated their rotations almost without thinking.

Then all of a sudden I heard a man's voice joining in. When I looked at one of the therapists, she looked stunned, and then smiled broadly while she stared at the man's back. Another therapist then stopped working the arms of the patient she was attending and listened intently. I soon realized they were totally surprised to hear the man's voice

I continued singing as I walked slowly to his side, and then saw his face. It was obvious he had had a rather debilitating stroke recently and his mouth was all contorted as he was "singing" the words to a hymn that obviously meant a great deal to him. The fact that the words were incoherent and the tune was all over the place did not matter at all, because he was being blessed by it.

When I finished it, I immediately started it all over once again. At that point he and I locked eyes and I smiled at him and patted his shoulder. And then, with considerable effort, he slowly stretched out his arm and took my hand. He then deliberately and painstakingly brought my hand up to his lips and kissed it. All the while I continued to sing and smile into his face.

By this time the head nurse had come to stand behind me so she could observe his reaction and his movements. When I turned to look at her, I noticed tears running down her cheeks as she, too, was smiling at him.

At that point I looked across the room and noticed that the woman who had requested the hymn was crying. Immediately I went to her and hugged her, thanking her for suggesting that particular hymn. She then whispered in my ear during the long hug, "Oh, how I needed that song today."

It was obvious that the staff and the patients and I had truly felt the same emotions in the past three or four minutes.

I smiled at all of them and as I headed for the door, I said to the patients and staff alike, "I would wish each of you a happy holiday weekend, but I think we have all just now observed the true meaning of Easter."

As I was driving home, still filled with the enormous meaning of what had just transpired in that room filled with all kinds of machines and equipment, the radio in my car was playing a most appropriate old hymn of passion, "When I Survey The Wondrous Cross." I listened to the words of the last two verses:

> *"See, from his head, his hands, his feet,*
> *sorrow and love flow mingled down.*
> *Did e'er such love and sorrow meet,*
> *or thorns compose so rich a crown?"*
>
> *"Were the whole realm of nature mine,*
> *that were an offering far too small;*
> *Love so amazing, so divine,*
> *demands my soul, my life, my all."*
> --Isaac Watts, 1707

> *As each one has received a gift, minister it to one another.*
> -- I Peter 4:10

> *A bird doesn't sing*
> *because he has an answer;*
> *He sings*
> *because he has a song.*
> -- Unknown

# Chapter Six

## *Irene*

The other day I was looking for a lady who had been in an extended care facility for several weeks.

I have visited Irene many times, and since we attend the same church, she loves it when I just open my hymnal and sing some of the old hymns. Usually we chat for a while when I first walk into her room, but it isn't long before she'll ask, "Aren't you going to sing something today?"

And I have never called on her but what her husband of over fifty years is sitting right there in her room with her. Sometimes they are discussing something they just read in the morning paper, and sometimes they are just in each other's presence. But seldom is the television turned on. It is just them, being together.

Most times I stop and sing to the residents who are in the physical therapy room as I walk down the various hallways. The staff loves that, because while the patients are singing along with me, they forget that the therapist is manipulating a painful joint in their leg or arm.

Since I had found Irene's room empty, I asked the nurse where I could find her, and she directed me to the therapy room. When I entered, she waved to me.

The staff said, "Here's the Singing Lady. She'll sing your favorite songs."

So we sang a couple of patriotic songs and a couple of hymns. The response was wonderful as we were really into our sing-a-long.

When I started to sing, "Let Me Call You Sweetheart," I looked over at Irene and smiled as she was singing. Then, suddenly she stopped as I could see she was looking behind me over my shoulder. When I turned to see who had entered, there was her husband coming through the doorway with his eyes fully on her. He was singing as if there was no one else in the room. By the time he slowly walked to her wheelchair, bent and kissed her on the cheek, most of the cheeks of most of the staff and patients alike were wet with tears.

As they sat together, holding hands, singing that song to each other, they were totally oblivious to anyone else being in the room.

On that morning, for no more than two minutes, the presence of true love was the best therapy in the entire world of medical care.

*Let me call you Sweetheart, I'm in love with you;*
*Let me hear you whisper that you love me, too.*
*Keep the love light glowing in your eyes so true,*
*Let me call you Sweetheart, I'm in love with you.*

-- Music by Leo Friedman
-- Lyrics by Beth Slater Whitson
1910

# Chapter Seven

## *Susan*

My lawyer-friend asked me one day if I would call on a client of his. She is one of his several pro-bono cases, who are the "forgotten" to society, and who have no family or friends to visit them. He said he tries to see her every couple of weeks or so in the nursing home where she resides. But, he admitted, as well intentioned as his plans, his busy court cases sometimes get in the way.

Since I already had a couple of patients in that particular care facility, I happily agreed to visit her also. He went on to tell me she is a 73-year-old woman who was born both physically and emotionally challenged, with her demeanor that of a young girl. Her speech is not very clear so she is a mostly solitary soul. Recently she had been put on Hospice care.

The first time I went to visit her, I was surprised by the starkness of her room. She was surrounded by four walls and the door I entered. There was nothing on the walls and the only personal item was an old picture of Susan sitting in her wheelchair next to Santa Clause. The nightstand next to her bed held the usual medical aids. The room was simply filled with the bed...and Susan.

She seemed startled that someone came to see her. I said, "Hi, Susan. My name is Judy, and I just thought I'd stop by and say hello."

She looked at me as if to say, "Why do you want to see me; you don't even know me."

Seeing that her lunch was mostly untouched on her tray table, I said, "Oh, chocolate pudding, my favorite. Do you want to eat yours while we chat?"

She obediently picked up her spoon and proceeded to play with the pudding.

I asked what her favorite dessert was and she mumbled, "Cookies". I continued asking her favorite things...colors, "Pink." Games she played as a child, "Hide and seek." And favorite song, to which she answered, "Every song." Little did I know how true that was. Before I left, I asked her if it was alright if I came back and maybe we would sing together.

She answered, "Tomorrow is OK."

When I returned, she noticed the hymnal I always carry with me and she asked, "Is that a Bible?"

I said, "No, it is my hymnal, and when you said you love all songs, I wanted to show you my favorite book of songs. I love to sing, do you?" Oh, her face brightened up, and her eyes were twinkling.

I started to sing "You Are My Sunshine", and immediately she joined in...loudly and with enthusiasm! While her speech was sometimes garbled, the words to the music she was singing were very clear.

When we finished, I started "Jesus Loves Me". Oh my! She put her head back on her pillow and belted it out. Even though she had uncontrollable shaking with the physical jerking of her whole body, she was looking upwards and waving her hands happily. When we finished (I thought), she immediately started singing the (little known) second verse, just staring at me to see if I knew the words, too. I did. And as we both continued singing, her face lit up and she flashed her toothless grin at me, as if to say, "You can be my new best friend if you want to."

Well, I stood there for forty minutes starting dozens of hymns and, after the first two or three words, she joined in on every one. I was stunned that she knew so many entire hymns, and it became a game with us. She knew she was impressing me and she kept saying, "I know 'em all. I know 'em all." Yep, she did. And that whole time we kept laughing out loud at the happy surprise we had discovered in each other.

Since she was wearing me out, I told her I needed to go. An immediate frown crossed her face and her arms began to wave around uncontrollably when she asked, "Are you ever gonna come back again?"

"Oh, yes," I answered as I said goodbye, "I want to find a hymn that you don't know."

Our pattern was established. With every visit, we talked a little and sang a lot. Sometimes, if she had them in, her ill-fitting false teeth would bob up and down in her mouth as she sang, but that never bothered her. She never stopped smiling while we sang.

One day as I was leaving, I bent down to hug her. She threw her arms around my neck and hugged me back hard, as she said in my ear, "I love you, Singing Lady."

As I straightened up, I smiled and said, "I love you, too." And as I turned to walk out of her room, I heard her saying, "I love you, three. I love you, four."

I quickly realized that somewhere in her unknown past, she had spent a lot of time in church. When she had been admitted to Hospice, the only information I had been given was that she had no known family or friends.

She was getting stronger, both physically and socially, every time I visited her. Her eating had improved and she even got to the point where she would wander up and down the halls, "motoring" her wheelchair with her feet and chatting with the other patients as she spent most of the time out of her room now.

Because she had improved so much, she no longer needed to be on Hospice service since the nursing staff in the extended care facility that had been her home for years could daily attend to her needs.

Well, she may no longer have been my official patient, but I was not about to stop visiting her. We were having too much fun.

One day several months later, I found her outside her door in the hall. I said, "Do you feel like singing today?" Silly question. So I started to push her wheelchair back into her room.

She got angry instantly and dug her heels into the floor. "I do not want to sing in my room, I want to sing out here." That was followed instantly by the command, "You start...now."

So I stood beside her chair and was thinking of something "quiet" to sing in the hall, but I guess I took too long for her because, all of a sudden, she threw her head back and belted out, "Yankee Doodle Came To Town", as she reached for my hand and started "propelling" herself, and me, down the hall.

I tried to get behind her and push the chair, so we wouldn't take up the whole space in the hall. But no. Quickly her temper flared again, as she reached back and insisted I walk beside her, not behind her. Okay.

At that point, I saw the nurses on duty smiling broadly as they turned sideways to get around us. We soon passed the doorway of another patient, and Susan said, "Come on, Phyllis, join us, we're having a parade." Like the proverbial Pied Piper, the parade increased in number, and it was no secret who was coming down the hall. The patients in their rooms and the staff all loved the ever-lengthening line of wheelchairs. We were now alongside the nurses' station and had just finished singing, "Amazing Grace", so I turned back and asked if any of the parade-members had a favorite song.

*One woman looked right at me and boldly started singing,*
*Show me the way to go home, I'm tired and I want to go to bed.*
*I had a little drink about an hour ago*
*and it went right to my head....*

Needless to say, the nurses, who were working on their charts, lowered their heads to the desk, shaking silently with uncontrollable laughter.

Another time, it had been over a week between visits and when I walked into her room, Susan said, plaintively, "Where were you? I have been 'singing' for you." (Translation, "I have been waiting for you so we can sing together.")



On a gloomy and dreary afternoon in the middle of December that same year, I brought a small, lighted Christmas tree and put it on the mostly-bare table at the foot of Susan's bed, next to the television set that had never been turned on. Ever. When I plugged the tree in, her eyes lit up and she started to clap.

I had also brought a pretty music box which played, "Jesus Loves

Me" when the lid was lifted. As I pulled the wrapped gift out of a sack, I said, "And what is Christmas without a present?"

Like a seven-year-old on Christmas morning, she held out her hands and ripped the paper, looked at the box, and then opened it to see what was inside. Except for the mechanism inside which made it work, it was empty! Her face fell like a stone because she didn't understand that the box was the gift and needed to be wound first in order to make it play. I quickly showed her how to wind this magic key on the bottom.

So I told her to open the box again. Sadly, she looked at me because she didn't want to see that emptiness again, so I reached over and lifted the lid. Immediately, she heard, "Jesus Loves Me", and she smiled with her whole face. Then I told her to close it, and, instantly, the music stopped, as sadness surrounded her again. After a few "practices", her eyes twinkled brighter than any of the lights on her little Christmas tree. She hollered, "Oh, Oh, Oh" in such a loud voice that a nurse came running into the room. Immediately the nurse saw me, and saw that Susan's cries were of delight and not of pain, as Susan showed the nurse how that box worked. Open. Shut. Open. Shut. She then held it up to the nurse and said, "Look what Mary brought me."

The nurse smiled and said, "No, Susan, her name is Judy."

Adamantly, Susan replied, "Her name is Mary and we love each other."

Trying to straighten her out, the nurse tried one more time, saying, "Susan, her name is Judy."

As she clung tightly to her new music box, Susan said, with all the certainty her mind could offer, "Her name is Mary – because she brought me Jesus."

I have no idea how I managed to breathe for the next couple of minutes. And, just as suddenly, Susan said to the nurse, "Will you put me in my rolling chair, please? I have to go and show my present to my friends." Then she looked at me and said, "I'll see you next time, Singing Lady." I had been dismissed.

When I got to the end of the hall, I looked back, and there was Susan, stopping in the doorways along her hall, opening and closing her magic box, and saying, "You wanna hear Jesus? Listen!"

For over a year, Susan continued to spend much of her day roaming the halls in her rolling chair, chatting with anyone who would talk with her. I continued to visit her as always. But as we were approaching our third year together, she began to gradually decline and was, once again, put back on Hospice.

As summer began to end, her days of freedom outside her room had also ended. Her discomfort increased and her appetite and energy decreased. She didn't sing as lustily, but she still managed to sing along some of the time. There were days when we would mostly just hold hands, happy to be in each other's presence.

However, each time I walked in, our greeting was the same, although much more subdued. Instead of her heartfelt hug around my neck, she would just give me her hand. I always started our visit singing *Jesus Loves Me* and sometimes she would look at the blank wall next to her bed, and say in a noticeably weaker voice, over and over again, "Jesus loves me. Jesus loves me. Jesus loves me." And then, as we were still holding hands, she would turn her head slowly and look at me and say, "I love Jesus most. And I love you next most."

One dreary autumn day, I walked in and the first thing I said was, "Susan, do you love to get presents?" I remembered her unbridled joy at opening her Christmas present that first year we were together.

Surprisingly, she perked up and even clapped her hands and answered, "Yes..., I love Jesus and I love you and I love presents!"

"Well, I have a present for you today. Do you like the color pink?"

"Yep. I love pink. I love Jesus and I love you and I love presents and I love pink."

So I covered her with a pink prayer shawl as she lay in the bed. She immediately made fists with all that pinkness inside both tightly closed hands. I said, "It is yours to keep forever and ever." She just kept kissing the shawl, that ordinary pink yarn which had been just a long, unending strand of yarn until I had knit it into a very special gift of love—for a very special Child of God. Her sweet spirit could still show joy. I just stood and watched that joy.

That day we really didn't need to talk because she kept caressing her new warm blanket as she was lost in the world of feeling and touching. After a couple of minutes I said, "Do you want to sing some of our favorite hymns."

Very quickly and very quietly she answered, "No, I am too busy now." I smiled and stood beside her a little while longer. I bent over and kissed her cheek and told her I would be back again soon, to which she quietly answered, "I know you will and you'll bring your songs, too, won't you?"

"Yep, I promise. I love you."

Happily she replied, "I love you, too. I love you three. I love you four." When I walked out of the suddenly-no-longer-dark-and-dingy room, I stood outside her door in the hall and watched her putting her fingers through every "hole" created by the pattern of stitches in her new shawl, with her eyes closed and a smile on her face. A picture-memory I will never forget.

As the next year moved along, Susan seemed to be much more agitated for reasons she could not verbalize. She spent all of her time in her bed, not even able to be put in her wheelchair to sit in the hall any more. With each visit, her room seemed to grow even smaller and darker. But the precious hymns we shared together were like soothing medicine even though she oftentimes didn't join in the singing any more. The light of Susan seemed to be dimming.

In December, I sang every Christmas carol I knew. Many times.

One day when I went to kiss her cheek in our "hello" greeting, she winced and said, "That hurt." As I looked more closely, I could see prominent bruises that went from her cheek down her neck. When I registered deep concern to the nursing staff, they admitted that she had fallen out of bed the day before.

A couple of days later, I again sang one Christmas Carol after another. It was a bit difficult when I sang the third verse of "Away in a Manger", thinking this might be the last time I would sing it to her....

*Be near me, Lord Jesus, I ask thee to stay*
*Close by me forever, and love me, I pray.*
*Bless all your dear children in thy tender care,*
*And fit us for heaven to live with thee there.*

A day or two later, I took her a Christmas present. I had knit a new blanket to put over her as she lay there so quietly now. After singing a couple of carols, I asked, "Susan, what is your very most favorite Christmas carol?"

Without hesitating, she said, "God Bless America!" Sweet Susan! So, I smiled and sang that beautiful patriotic song while she smiled and "conducted" me with her hand.

Ten days after the appearance of her bruises, I walked into her room one snowy morning and almost stepped on her as she lay on a mattress on the floor. She was sleeping so I went to the nurse's station immediately, only to learn that, once again, she had fallen. So the decision had been made that, for her safety she would spend the rest of her life lying on the floor. It so hurt my heart at the thought and sight of that, even though I knew it was for her safety. Also, I could see in her eyes and into her fragile mind, that she couldn't understand why her "Mary", her "Singing Lady", her "mother figure", no longer kissed her or touched her or held her hand, because my 77-year old bones just didn't allow me to get down on the floor...and get back up again.

After that I went to see her most every day, including Christmas Eve and Christmas morning.

As usual on New Year's Day, I was deep into putting away my Christmas decorations and starting the mandatory deep cleaning of the "December dust" which gathers around and under those pretties that bring sparkle to our homes.

The weather forecast was daunting as it kept warning of a fierce winter storm, so I chose to listen to the last of the holiday music while I worked. And then the phone rang late in the afternoon. It was the nursing home telling me, "Susan is actively dying." In the fading light of the first day of the new year, I looked out the window at the encroaching darkness and wetlooking streets. The four miles between that nursing home and me seemed like going across country. But my deep desire that my sweet Susan not be alone as she was walking down the path to Heaven led me to put on my Hospice jacket, grab my hymnal, and, with faith that Jesus was leading me, I went to her room and sat down on the floor beside her.

There was no response but I knew she could still feel my kiss, hear my voice, and hold my hand. I told her how much I loved her, and thanked her for challenging me to remember every word of every verse of every hymn we ever sang. I tried to sing, but could only manage a squeak as the tears fell down my cheeks. I knew she wouldn't mind if I cried, because she knew they were tears of love for the memories we had made together. I managed to sing "You Are My Sunshine", while outside the darkness had fallen, and inside her room the light of Heaven was becoming more bright.

I tried to sing again, and this time the gift of song was there—from God to me to her. I sang hymn after hymn. I prayed as I stroked her forehead thanking Jesus out loud for the happy journey we had taken for over three years and how excited her eyes would get when we talked about the first time Jesus would hug her in Heaven. And how beautiful it would be as she could walk freely down the beautiful paths to the unending flower gardens which led me to sing, "In The Garden", one of her favorites.

I kissed her again and said, "Sweetheart, I'll see you again, either here or in Heaven. But I have to go home now because it is dark and snowing. And you are almost Home now, too, where it will be bright and sunny forever. Our Jesus will see both of us home safely."

Before I rang for the nurse to come and help me up off the floor, I sang the third verse of "Away In A Manger". And then the last song she heard on earth was her "bestest one", "Jesus Loves Me." I remembered the many, many times she insisted on singing that second verse and how she would hold her hands up to the sky, to be sure Jesus was listening to us...

*"Jesus loves me, He who died, Heaven's gates to open wide.*
*He will take away my sins; Let this little child come in.*
*Yes, Jesus loves me, Yes Jesus loves me,*
*Yes, Jesus loves me, the Bible tells me so."*

Her favorite verse of her favorite song was becoming a reality.

Before the light of day the next morning, I went out to get the paper and I knew immediately that my plan to go see her was impossible because of a huge snow drift in front of my garage door. I called the nurse's station at 6 a.m. They said she had had a peaceful night. I told them I could not get there until my driveway was plowed out, and they again said they would call me if she entered the Gates of Heaven before I got there.

A couple hours later they called. The call was short. As I sat in my chair, still holding the phone in my hand, saddened because of a snow drift that kept me from my desire that she not die alone, I found myself smiling...because she wasn't alone. Jesus had come and led her to peace.

Somewhat subdued, I was eating my lunch when my doorbell rang. There stood a delivery man holding a very large something wrapped in several layers of opaque plastic, protecting the heavy item from the weather.

When I placed it on the counter in the kitchen and opened the covering, I saw a beautiful large Peace plant. I will never forget the feeling that washed over me as I opened the card...just four hours after that phone call. It read,

*Thank you for being there for me and so many others in song and spirit. I felt your presence as I went to Heaven and didn't want you to drive in the snow. Blessings on you. Love, Susan*

*I have shown you in every way that you must support the weak.*
*He said 'It is more blessed to give than to receive.'*
-- Acts 20:35

*Thank you, my Lord, for giving me the opportunity*
*to love and to be loved.*
-- JB

# Chapter Eight

## *Bruce*

The phone rang.

When I answered, the weeping voice of my long-time friend said, "Bruce just died."

Every day for the past few weeks I had called his bedside in a Hospice facility in another state to sing his favorite hymn, *The Old Rugged Cross*. At first his weakened baritone voice had joined me as the phone lay on his pillow. But for the last several days he had silently listened as our "congregation of four" had surrounded his bedside while my friend, his wife, and their son had held the phone to his ear as I sang to him.

One day several weeks earlier, he had asked me what day it was. I told him it was Sunday. He said softly, "Oh, how I miss church." After that, every day "church" came to him via our phone visits.

The volunteering of hymns and prayers were lovingly channeled through the magic of technology via the phone from 1,000 miles away as the peace of Jesus filled one small room where the focal point was a bed holding a dying man as he took his last breaths on earth before walking through the Gates of Heaven.

*As we have opportunity, let us do good to everyone.*

-- Galatians 6:10

*The people who are truly happy*
*Are those who seek—and find—ways to serve others.*

-- Albert Schweitzer

# Chapter Nine

## *Beverly*

One day I asked our visitation minister for a list of those folks who reside in our local nursing homes. I figured that when I was making my usual calls on my Hospice patients, I could also stop in to visit with our church members from time to time.

After seeing my patients in one of our nursing homes one day, I went down the hall to see one of the names on the list...someone I had never met before. Of course, she looked skeptical to see a stranger walk into her room, especially as I stood there in my official Hospice jacket. I introduced myself saying that we were members of the same church.

The expression on her face changed immediately, and she even began to get a little agitated. I realized it wasn't the Hospice jacket that bothered her, but was the fact that we went to the same church.

Not one to be easily discouraged, I asked her how long she had been a member of our church, and she said, "I guess that depends because I don't think I belong there anymore."

I said, "Oh, that is why I am here. You know, one of our ministers has just moved and another of our ministers died very suddenly a month ago. So, I am just stopping in to see you so that you will know that, while we are going through these changes with our staff, you are still being remembered and prayed for."

That struck a chord in her and she said, "I didn't know that anyone there remembered me. You see several years ago one of my daughters died of cancer, and I just couldn't bring myself to go back to church for a long time. Then I tried to attend again for a while, but it was too hard. I couldn't do it because of the memories going there brought back to me. So my other daughter (who also belongs to our church) called the church office and requested a minister to call on me. One day a couple of months later, the phone rang and this minister (I can't remember his name), introduced himself and said, 'I know I should have called on you long ago, but you know how large our church is, and I guess you are just one of those who have fallen through the cracks'. When I realized that I wasn't any more important to my church than that, I just hung up the phone. I didn't need to hear him say that my years of faithfulness was only worthy of 'falling through the cracks' now that I am older and in a nursing home. I have never heard from anyone in that church again...until you just now walked into my room."

I bent down to her sitting in her wheelchair and hugged her for the longest time. When I stood up again, we both had tears running down our cheeks.

She saw that I was carrying my hymnal (which is all marked up like most folks' Bibles,) and then she said, "Are you a minister?"

I quickly replied, "Oh, no, I am just an ordinary child of God, just like you are. I just love to come and sing the old, old hymns to my patients (as I pointed to my bright blue jacket), and I thought I would simply stop in and say hello to you."

I then asked her what her favorite old hymn was, and she quickly answered, "The Old Rugged Cross", so I sang it to her as we both found those tears running down our cheeks again. And we again hugged each other, as she said to me, "Tell me again, why did you come to see me?"

I said, "Well, the Shepherd (Jesus) arranged for me to find the list of the sheep in our church who are lonely. And I guess He led me to find you this afternoon because HE knew you have been a lost lamb. But, dear Beverly, you are not lost any more. I am sure that someone from our church is going to stop by and see you much more often after today...if only to remind you that you are very important to us—and always have been. And not only as a member of our church, and as a volunteer of the compassionate organization of Hospice, I can assure you that I already feel our care and concern for each other today is the beginning of a lovely friendship. Until you tell me to stop, you can be assured that I will stop in and visit with you often!"

One day, shortly after I arrived for my weekly visit with her, the nurse walked into her room and announced that it was time to give Beverly her shower. My friend replied to the nurse, "Oh, please come back another time because my church just came to visit with me."

And the amazing end to this story is that for the past almost three years now, we have shared a comfortable, happy, and loving friendship. Together we wandered back fifty years to when we were young mothers, raising children, cooking meals from scratch, spending hours ironing, and gardening in the heat of summer. We always ended up laughing at this "new generation," and agreed with each other that they don't have a clue to what real work is.

Whenever I hugged her goodbye, I always said "I'll be back soon so we can continue to try and solve the problems of today's modern world by sharing the memories of those good old days, and the journey that we both walked before we met."

NOTE: One Sunday I stopped by to see Beverly after church, and didn't have my Hospice jacket on. When I entered the room, she took one look at me and said, "Hey, you forgot to finish getting dressed this morning." I realized quickly that my jacket had become a sign of compassion and comfort to her.

*Therefore, comfort one another.*

-- I Thessalonians 5:11

*The bonus gift of volunteering*
*is that, as you serve others,*
*many times a friendship begins.*

--JB

# Chapter Ten

## *Kathleen*

Oftentimes, when I would make my calls in the nursing home, I would visit with the roommate of my patient as well. I would usually hug my patient before I left, and it was not unusual for me to hug the roommate, too.

After several years visiting, singing, and praying with my patient, Beverly, she peacefully entered into the Gates of Heaven. I knew her roommate, Kathleen, would be lonely, so I would stop in and visit with her from time to time.

As I was walking down the hall one day, I stopped in to see Kathleen, only to notice that there was now a new person in the bed where Beverly used to lie.

While we were chatting, Kathleen said to me, "My new roommate is so lonely, would you please hug her like you hugged me before you even knew my name?"

The gift of a hug is a blessing that just keeps on growing.

*So then, as we have opportunity, let us do good to all men...*
-- Galatians 6:10

*Never underestimate the power of the human touch.*
-- Unknown

# Chapter Eleven

## *Arthur*

As I was walking up the sidewalk to the Hospice Center one lovely spring day, I saw the Minister of Visitation from my church walking toward me. We greeted each other, and he asked, "Are you here to sing to Arthur?"

I looked quizzically at him, and answered that I was going to see a patient of mine. He then told me that a member of our church had been admitted and asked if I would sing to him.

When I approached his wife, Millie, standing alone in the hall just outside his room, I smiled as I greeted her. Since her attendance at worship services had been sporadic in the past few years, due to her husband's illness, we really didn't know each other. I had heard their name and that was all.

As we were walking into his room, I noticed his eyes were open as he lay on his side facing the window, but he was not moving. She immediately went to his bedside and began to lovingly stroke his face as I asked if either of them had a favorite old hymn they might like me to sing. Without missing a beat, she said, "His favorite hymn is 'Faith of Our Fathers'". I made a mental note to myself that no one had ever before requested that song to be sung as life was ebbing away.

When I was done, I then sang her favorite, along with a couple others, and she and I chatted for a short time before I left, saying I would be happy to come back another time if she would like. She said that would be fine.

Since I really didn't know them all that well, and I usually don't return for a few days, unless I am asked to return sooner, it seemed strange to me that the next day I just couldn't forget that "scene" from the day before. I was singing to myself while I was ironing that morning, and felt strongly that I should return to the Hospice Center. I unplugged the iron before finishing that chore, put on my Hospice jacket, grabbed my hymnal, and entered that hospice room about fifteen minutes later.

Millie looked as surprised to see me as I was to have felt the urgency to return. She greeted me warmly and introduced me to her daughter who was standing on the other side of the bed. She then said, "Are you going to sing again? My husband loves music, as do I."

I smiled and said I had been thinking of them and just wanted to come and share some more hymns, if that would be of comfort to her. I had noticed that his hospital bed had been lowered to the floor on this day, so, when I started to sing, she got out of the chair and knelt down beside him, again caressing his face.

I just casually flipped through the hymnal singing whatever I found on the page that opened up. After sharing about three old songs, a seldom sung, very short hymn appeared in my random selection which contains beautifully simple words, so I stood there and sang:

*Turn your eyes upon Jesus;*
*Look full in His wonderful face.*
*And the things on earth will grow slowly dim*
*In the light of His glory and grace.*

When I was done, Millie looked up at me from her position on the floor, and I noticed the most amazingly beautiful smile as tears were running down her cheeks. Since it was obvious that the song had meant something to her, I began to sing it again...

"Turn your eyes upon Jesus;
Look full in His..."

Arthur took a very obvious, audible breath...his last, as he peacefully entered the gates of Heaven.

I knew right away that he had died, and within only a few seconds the nurse was in the room. I went to Millie and hugged her hard, and said if she needed anything to be sure and call me. I also hugged their daughter who had been holding her father's hand during the sharing of these hymns.

The profound intimacy of peace and silence as the sun had streamed into that room on that lovely April morning truly surrounded me as I drove home immediately after that. What an honor to have been able to share the beauty of Arthur passing peacefully from this earth into his eternal home in those few moments we had quietly shared together.

I cannot express the emotion I felt when, a day later, the phone rang and a dear friend of Arthur's called me. He said the two of them had been wonderful friends for many years. He wanted to thank me for the experience of the day before. He went on to say, "Millie told me about the last song that he heard as he slipped into the next life. Did you know that Arthur had been totally blind for the past six years?"

I struggled to maintain my composure as I humbly answered, "No, I did not know he was blind." At that moment, I understood Millie's beautiful smile as tears ran down her cheeks in that last precious minute of her husband's life. Of all the hymns in my beloved hymnal, I was led to sing...

*Turn your eyes upon Jesus;*
*Look full in His wonderful face.*
*And the things on earth will grow slowly dim*
*In the light of His glory and grace.*

NOTE: According to the friend who called me, Arthur had professed to be an agnostic most of his life. And yet, I smile when I realize how quickly Millie told me the name of her husband's favorite hymn. Both life, and death, are truly an amazing journey.

*Each of you should use whatever gift you have received to serve others.*
-- I Peter 4:10

*A big part of volunteering is listening to God's voice –*
*going where He wants you to go*
*and*
*doing what He wants you to do.*
-- JB

# Chapter Twelve
## *Mabel*

The effects of a stroke had taken away Mabel's speech. As she lay in her bed in the nursing home, I could see that rheumatoid arthritis had also been a part of her life for many years.

Her eyes smiled at me when I first entered her room, and I was also glad to see her son sitting beside her. I greeted both of them. After chatting with her son for a few minutes, I asked him if he knew what his mother's favorite hymn might be, as I had checked my notes to see that she had been very active in her church at one time.

Without hesitation, he replied, "He Touched Me", and Mabel's eyes smiled once again. Mother and son held hands as I sang that meaningful song.

The next few times I visited her, Mabel was alone so I imagined her son was working. One day, I was delighted to see him again, sitting faithfully beside her, holding her hand. He seemed to be unusually quiet so I just sang a few other hymns after singing "her" song.

As I was singing "Amazing Grace", I noticed tears dropping onto his chest. When I finished, he looked up at me and said, "Through all the rough times of my life, through all the worry I caused my Mom when I was lost, she never lost her amazing grace of faith that I would find my way back. If Mom could talk, she would have wanted you to sing that song in this room right now, today, when I am here, too."

I asked him if he might want a hug. He stood and let me hold him for several minutes. We never said a word. We just hugged. As I left, I said, "And may the amazing grace of Jesus bring you both peace today, and all the todays to come."

The next day Mabel entered the Gates of Heaven.

*Share with God's people who are in need. Practice hospitality.*
-- Romans 12:13

*The touch of His hand on mine!*
*Oh, the touch of His hand on mine!*
*There is grace and power in each lonely hour*
*In the touch of His hand on mine.*
-- Jessie Brown Pounds, 1913

# Chapter Thirteen

## *George*

The residents in the retirement community where I sing during their breakfast every Friday morning are friendly and responsive. Sometimes they join me in the singing of old songs, old hymns, old patriotic songs. Sometimes they just eat quietly and sometimes their faces tell me they are remembering a life long ago as their memories go back to the days when they were young.

I have missed only a handful of these weekly Friday morning visits together in the eight years that I have visited them in their lovely, bright dining room. After singing together, I visit every table and chat with each resident individually.

One week in early Spring, I chose to sing songs that reminded us of the promise and beauty of nature. In between the songs, I shared with them some of the local sights of flowers and bushes that had seemed to come to life in the week since we had last met.

I made my way to a corner table by the windows and greeted each resident, asking one of the men how his past week had been.

"I'm not doing very well." I had noticed that George's wife had not been at the table the week before, nor was she there again this day. The absence of her wheelchair sitting beside him was very obvious.

I asked George where his wife was and very softly, he said, "She isn't going to make it. She's dying."

George had comforted many people during his career as a funeral director. I put my arms around him to now offer comfort to him. "Is she upstairs in your room? Would it help if I went and softly sang her favorite old hymn?" I had remembered how she would listen intently each week and often times she would softly join in the singing.

"No, she is in the hospital. I don't have a car any more to go and see her, but would you go see her?"

Immediately, I assured him that I would honor his request that very morning.

As I continued to stand with my arm around his shoulder, he stared at his plate which still held most of his breakfast. Then, he looked up at me and said "Forty-two years, forty-two years, and now this."

I smiled back at him and said, "And the joy of those memories is just a sample of the joy you two will have when you meet again in Heaven. When you see her again, she will be pain-free and able to walk with you again."

He abruptly looked me square in the eyes and said, "How do you know that?"

Very quickly I replied, "I saw you smile a couple of times when we were talking about the signs of spring that have filled our lives this past week. Brown, lifeless grass is turning into a lush green carpet covering everything. Seemingly dead branches on the trees are bursting into the fat buds which surprise us each morning with more color as they begin to open. Flowering bushes and bright flowers make us smile as they pop up everywhere. Everything that appeared dead has burst into new life. Surely our Lord cares more for your wife, and for all of us, than He does for a blade of grass or a dandelion, or a tulip."

He listened to every word, and finally said, "Do you promise?"

I smiled and said, "Better than that, our Lord promises."

We continued looking at each other and finally his face relaxed as he squeezed my hand and said with such simplicity, "Thank you. I feel better now."

*Do not withhold good from those who deserve it,*
*when it is in your power to help them.*
-- Proverbs 3:27

GRIEF
Grief has no rule book.
Grief has no time frame.
Grief is as individual as a fingerprint.

The only people who think
there is a time limit for grief,
have never lost a piece of their heart.

When mourning the death of a loved one,
take all the time you need.
-- JB

# Chapter Fourteen

## *Beth*

Today I was blessed with a few minutes of unexpected joy while walking down the hall of a nursing home.

Having just visited and sung with one of my patients, I noticed a small woman in a sitting area across the hall. She had that morning's newspaper in her lap as she motioned for me to go over to her.

I had never seen her before, and we smiled as I approached. She looked up at me and said, "May I be so bold as to ask you a favor? I heard you singing and would you please sing *Jesus Loves Me*?"

So I took her hand and sang as her face lit up with joy. When I finished, she said, "I know He does, but I just needed to hear it."

I sat in the empty chair beside her and said, "Oh, yes, He does. He knows your name, and He knows your heart, and He loves you as if you are the only person in His universe." So I immediately sang several old hymns, all of which she knew. She mouthed the words with me as her lined and wrinkled face radiated the joy of this unexpected meeting of two strangers.

We chatted for only a couple more minutes, mostly about the beauty of the hymns. She told me she liked to sit in that chair and watch her limited world of life in the nursing home go by, silently blessing those patients who seemed to be much worse off than she.

Then she sweetly dismissed me by opening her arms as she looked up at me and said, "Before you go on your way, do you also have an extra hug?"

Oh, did I! I told her that I believed the main reason God gave us arms was so we could hug each other.

And as I turned to continue on my rounds, I assured her that she had given me the best gift I would have all day, a new friend. I promised her that I would sing "Jesus Loves Me" to her a couple times a week, each time I visited that particular nursing home. She smiled and said, "My name is Beth and, just in case I am resting, you can find me in Room 211."

With a smile, we waved goodbye to each other. As I was leaving the facility about thirty minutes later, I saw her walking down her hall, noticeably limping with great effort as she pushed her walker slowly toward Room 211.

*Give, and it will be given to you.*
-- Luke 6:38

*Not all of us can do great things.*
*But we can do small things with great love.*
-- Mother Teresa

# Chapter Fifteen

## *Emma*

What a treat I had in store for me when I met Emma!

All I knew when I went to see her the first time was that she was a "failure to thrive" patient who lived in the home she had occupied for many decades. Her 24/7 caregiver met me at the door on that warm summer day, and my first impression was what a tiny house it was tucked in among other small homes in a very old neighborhood.

As I entered the bedroom, that first impression was confirmed. The hospital bed, which consumed the room, had to be positioned at an angle in order to fit the space of a room which didn't even contain a closet.

There in that little room with the big bed lay the tiniest woman I had ever seen. She seemed to melt into the sheets of the bed, but when she smiled at me, space didn't matter! I introduced myself to her as I took her hand at the bedside, and from then on, I belonged to her. I was putty in her hands!

Her toothless grin and, even though her eyesight was gone, her dancing eyes belied the fact that she was 107 years old. And, right away she asked me how old I was! I laughed at that and answered, "Well, I haven't been able to say this for many, many years, but I am young enough to be your daughter!"

She laughed back at me and said, "Well, I didn't have one of those, so you'll do just fine." She then looked at the red book I was carrying with so many turned-down pages, bookmarks, and sticky notes poking out on every side, and asked, "Is that your Bible?"

"No, it's my hymnal which speaks to me much like a Bible."

"Well, then, honey, let's get to singing."

I knew we had already become best friends. I think we had been together all of three minutes at that point. "Emma," I said, "what is your favorite hymn?"

Immediately she shot back the answer, "All of them."

I started to sing, and after the first hymn, she said, "That was my favorite." I sang another one. Same response when I finished: "That was my favorite." I smiled and started to chat some more when she interrupted, "Keep singing, honey." Since she had begun to sing, fast and loud, along with me, I began another one... "On a hill far away" (with her voice drowning me out), "stood an old rugged cross, the…", and immediately in the next breath she started, "Beneath the Cross of Jesus," and I quickly started to follow her lead, but when she got to the word "Jesus", she again abruptly changed the song to "Jesus loves me, this I know…" and then, upon singing the word "know", her mind once again shifted gears, and out came, "I know that my Redeemer liveth."

I couldn't help it. I laughed right out loud as I tried to keep up with her. She then began to laugh, too. I bent down to hug her and embrace the joy of that moment!

She was so anxious to sing those songs she loved so dearly that she couldn't get them out of her mouth fast enough. As frail as she was, I knew I shouldn't stay any longer, so as not to tire her out. I said, "I have so enjoyed spending time with you, but I really must go now."

She looked up at me and said, while pointing to my hymnal, "But, honey, you haven't sung them all yet," as if she thought I would go through the entire hymnal!

The next time I went to see her, she was asleep, but the caregiver assured me that she would want me to wake her up. This is always a tricky decision, because oftentimes a patient is the most peaceful when they are sleeping. But I did wake her up, and in the few seconds that it took for her to realize who I was, her face brightened up that little room like a steady ray of sunshine. I said, "I came to sing again."

Her immediate response was, "Why have you been gone so long?" I had been there the day before.

We thoroughly enjoyed each other's presence once again, and thus began our singing marathon which would continue for the next several visits. As I was getting ready to leave that second day, I said, "I'll be back to see you, Emma."

"When?"

"Well, soon."

"When is soon?"

"In another day or two," I answered.

"Well, honey, don't wait too long. I'm 107, you know."

It was becoming more and more noticeable that she was getting weaker and weaker with each visit. She loved it when I held her hand, which I did most of the time. But I could almost feel her energy fading. I knew Jesus was calling her when she said one day, "Honey, I think I am just going to listen to you today."

One month and one day after I met her, I got a phone call from the Hospice Center asking me if I was planning to go and see her that day because she was actively dying. I assured them that I was, but when the phone rang, I was just walking out the door to go to the cardiologist to have a stress test. I knew I had to have that test, because I had surgery scheduled for the following week. I had no choice. I asked the nurse who called me to please call the caregiver and explain that I would be there as soon as I could.

When my medical test was completed, I went out into the warm sunshine and prayed that Emma was still waiting for one more song. The caregiver answered the door immediately with tears running down her cheeks as she hugged me and whispered in my ear, "She is waiting for you."

I went to her bedside immediately and took her little hand in both of mine and said, "Oh, Emma, I am so glad you waited because I want to be with you when you see Jesus' face for the first time." Very softly, I started to sing...

*Abide with me; fast falls the even-tide;*
*In life, in death, O Lord, abide with me.*

I sang all the way through to the last line of one of her beloved hymns. And with my own tears filling my eyes, I sang another...

*Just as I am, thou wilt receive,*
*wilt welcome, pardon, cleanse, relieve;*
*Because thy promise I believe,*
*O Lamb of God, I come, I come.*

Knowing that soon she would be able to see again, and sing her beloved hymns for all of eternity, I then sang...

*Amazing grace! How sweet the sound*
*that saved someone like me!*
*I once was lost, but now am found;*
*was blind, but now I see.*

Her breathing was so faint at this point that there was no movement of the sheet any more. The most appropriate hymn to sing as her long life ended filled that little room with one more favorite...

*Softly and tenderly Jesus is calling,*
*calling for you and for me;*
*See on the portals he's waiting and watching,*
*watching for you and for me.*
*Come home, come home;*
*you who are weary, come home;*
*Earnestly, tenderly, Jesus is calling,*
*calling Oh, loved one, come home!*

This beautiful lady whose husband died many years earlier, who never had any children, and who lived in the family home all of her life, had a wealth of people waiting for her in Heaven. On earth, she was a woman of great character, deep faith, and resilient optimism according to a feature article in the local paper after she died. But to me, she was one of the most contented people I had ever met. I told her once that I want to be just like her when I grow up! And I can still hear her laugh and see those dancing eyes.

The unexpected blessings one receives from volunteering far outweigh what we give.

A sweet 107-year old woman whom I visited many times in the short month that I knew her loved singing old hymns with me. I initially went to minister to her. But one day in her frail voice, which was just above a whisper, she said, "I pray for you all the time."

She was volunteering to fill my soul with her prayers, when all the time I thought I was the one doing the volunteering.

*Don't forget to be kind to strangers, for bu dpomg sp. some who have done this have entertained angels without realizing it.*
-- Hebrews 13:2

*If you ever need a helping hand, it is at the end of your arm. As you get older you must remember you have a second hand. The first one is to help yourself. The second hand is to help others.*
-- Audry Hepburn

# Chapter Sixteen

## *Bert*

Once in a while a visit may not be too pleasant, but it can turn out to be productive. Such was the case when a long-time neighbor of mine was sent to a nursing home when the insurance for his hospitalization had run out. It had been determined that physical therapy was needed before he could return home.

Bert was not happy. His nature was to always be in control. He did not want to be there, and as soon as I entered his room, he looked at me and said, "Go away, Judy."

Since he was a man of few words, at first I thought he was joking. He was not. I smiled and said, "I just thought you might want some company for a few minutes."

"Well, I don't, so just go home."

Again, I realized his demeanor was not the pleasant Bert that I had always known. So, as I was putting my coat back on, and turned to leave his room, I said, "Are you eating and doing your exercises?"

He shot back at me, "I don't like the food here, and nobody can make me exercise."

As I was almost at the door, I quietly said, "Well, I guess I won't need to hurry back then, because the longer you don't eat or go to therapy, the longer you will be here."

I paused to wave to him, and he said, "OK, Judy, you win. You said the magic words. Tell the nurse to bring my lunch tray back on your way out."

Three days later, I went back and found him in the physical therapy room. He still had not found his pleasant disposition, and so I simply said I just wanted to stop and say hello on my way to the grocery store. He just grunted and went back to his leg lifts.

He went home in less than two weeks. And the next time I saw him, he deliberately came up to me, gave me a hug, and said simply, "Thanks, Judy, I needed that." Still a man of few words, but his hug said it all.

Sometimes visiting those in need seems like the wrong thing to do, but then sometimes visiting those in need is the right thing to do. Eventually most folks realize that an act of kindness means that someone cares.

*...let us love, not in word or speech, but in truth and action.*
-- I John 3:18

*Let your light shine before others, so that they may see your good works and give glory to your Father in heaven.*
-- Matthew 5:16

# Chapter Seventeen

## *Greta*

Her name was Greta. I had visited her for five years. She was a sweet lady, but I learned quickly that she also wanted the world to turn according to her wishes. She was possessive in that whenever I went to see her, I best spend more time with her than with other patients. She lived in a private home which had been converted to a home for the elderly. She kept track of how long I sang to, and visited with the other residents, making sure I didn't look at the clock when I went in to chat with her!

She loved to tell stories and I loved to listen. We enjoyed laughing together, and she always had a different "favorite" hymn she wanted me to sing every time I walked through her door. She so wanted to stump me by requesting one I might not know.

Greta was 95, and in remarkably good health, with an endearing quick wit. She dressed every day as if she were going to be attending high tea in the afternoon. She kept current on the news and was a voracious reader. She and her husband had married quite late in life. He had died many years ago, when they were both in their eighties. At the time of his last illness, a visiting nurse had asked her one day, "Do you have children?"

And without skipping a beat, she quickly replied, "No, but we're working on it."

A couple months ago, a vicious bout of flu visited countless numbers of people in our area, including Greta. She was taken to the hospital, and I found her in the ICU area, hooked up to so many machines. Slowly she opened her eyes and spoke through the heavy-duty breathing device, "I knew you'd find me." I sang several of her favorite hymns and returned to her bedside every day. Even though she had lapsed into a coma, I still sang to her.

A couple of weeks later, I was making my usual rounds visiting my patients, and as I pulled up to the private home where she and three other patients stayed, I noticed an ambulance in the driveway. Quickly I rushed inside. To my delight, I found Greta had regained consciousness and demanded to be brought back to what had been her home for the past few years. As they were settling her back into her bed, I visited with the other folks in the residence.

When I entered Greta's room, it was obvious that she was about to reunite with her husband in Heaven before long. I went to her bedside and took her hand, and as she opened her eyes, she said in such a weak voice, "Oh, Judy, I knew you'd be here when I got home." (Actually, I had no idea she had regained consciousness in the hospital that morning and was being brought back to her home.) I stood there as we both smiled at each other while holding hands. She was so peaceful in this last journey. It was truly the grace of God that I was there at that moment.

It was an effort for her to talk, so as I held her hand, I sang a hymn. She had always said that whatever hymn I was singing was her favorite! In the warmth and peace of this little room, she looked at me when I was finished, squeezed my hand, and said, "I have never told you my real very favorite hymn I want to hear you sing:

*Praise to the Lord, the Almighty, the King of creation!*
*O my soul praise him, for he is thy health and salvation!*
*All ye who hear, now to his temple draw near;*
*Join me in glad adoration!*

As I sang, we both felt the presence of our Jesus in that room. She had truly praised Him her entire life long. When I finished, she almost whispered, "We'll meet again In the Garden in Heaven. Praise God, I'm almost there. But you have to promise me something. You still have miles to go. Promise me that you'll keep on praising Him until we meet again."

I kissed her forehead and, looking deep into her eyes, I said, "I promise".

Letting go of her hand, I walked into the hall and wept. Mingled with tears of the sadness at the loss of yet another friend were tears of joy at the beauty of sharing the true meaning of making a friend of a stranger, when life's journey is winding down.

*It is God himself who has made us what we are and given us new lives from Jesus Christ; and long ages ago He planned that we should spend our lives in helping others.*
-- Ephesians 2:10

*Our life is like a rainbow.*
*At the one end of the colorful arc,*
*where heaven and earth touch,*
*we begin our journey.*
*We take our first breath of the unknown beauty ahead.*
*We increase in brightness as we move upward toward middle age.*
*We begin to fade and lose vibrancy as we descend,*
*until at the other end of the colorful arc,*
*where heaven and earth touch,*
*we end our journey.*
-- JB

# Chapter Eighteen

## *Marilyn*

Not all of my patients are elderly.

My phone rang about four o'clock on a sunny Mother's Day Sunday afternoon. I didn't think it was one of my children because the ones who live out of town had already called to exchange loving greetings and, as always, take a walk down memory lane to years long gone when they were young. Now their children had children of their own, and I love listening to them tell their own stories of being grandparents.

The voice on the other end of the line was a sweet lady who works at the beautiful Hospice Center which is located only about five miles from my home. Kathryn said, "Judy, I surely hope I am not interrupting your Mother's Day gathering."

I assured her that she was not. I had been emptying the dishwasher as I was remembering the joy of the previous few hours spent with those of my family who live close enough to all get together on special days.

So Kathryn went on to tell me that a young 39-year-old mother, enduring the final stages of cancer, had just been admitted, and wondered if I could go and sing to her. The information on her chart revealed that she had been a very active church member before she became too ill to attend any longer.

Imagine my surprise when I entered her room ten minutes later.

There, on the floor at the foot of her hospital bed was her six year old son, contentedly playing with his toy cars. I greeted her, also saying hello to her mother who was sitting beside her. When I also smiled at the little boy, he shyly looked back at the parade of trucks and cars he was lining up beside him.

Immediately I was cognizant of the fact that there would be no more Mother's Days when these three generations would be together, as a hole was about to become a reality in the middle of that family's lineage.

I chatted for a few minutes with the two women and noticed that Marilyn, while very friendly, tired easily at talking. I did ask her favorite hymn, and she quickly said, "The Old Rugged Cross". As I started to softly sing that meaningful old hymn, the little boy looked up at his grandma as if to ask if that were permissible. She smiled her response to him by nodding. I realized he had been guided to be rather quiet when around his mother in these past few weeks.

When I finished, I asked the grandmother, Jenny, if she had a special song in which she found comfort, and without hesitating, she answered, "Because He Lives". As I stood there singing that lovely Gaither hymn, the words of the last verse became even more fitting in that room, knowing the journey those three generations were taking for their last time all together...

One morning, a couple of days later, I went to visit them again. Since Marilyn was asleep, I had a nice visit with her mother, who welcomed me warmly after our initial meeting. Tommy wasn't in the room this time, and Jenny told me that if I waited until late afternoon to visit, then Tommy would be there, too. The boy's uncle would pick him up at school and drive him to spend the rest of the day with his mom and grandma. Due to a divorce, Tommy was being raised by his mother alone. Jenny seemed to just want someone to talk to, so I listened until she then said, "Will you please sing some more old hymns?" So for almost an hour, she and I sang together whatever she picked out as her favorites from my hymnal.

I deliberately went to visit them the next afternoon because I seemed to be drawn to that quiet, contented, very well-behaved little boy. As usual, I greeted each of them, and this time Marilyn was awake. She, too, wanted a hug after her mother had quickly stood up to hug me as I walked in the room. Tommy watched this exchange of happy greetings and hugs, but I could tell he was still quietly considering this stranger who seemed to be friends with his mother and grandmother.

Jenny was anxious to "get to the music", so she interjected right away her request for our first hymn. Marilyn sang a few lines with us, but her weariness got the better of her, so she just listened. Then I looked down at Tommy and said, "I think I know a song that you know, too." And I started to sing "Jesus Loves Me".

The look on his face was priceless as he looked at his grandmother, thinking *How does she know the song that we sing in our Sunday school class?* I asked him if he knew it, and he timidly nodded his head yes, wondering how in the world an old woman like me could know his song. Once again I sang it, and when his mother and his grandma joined in, he eventually did, too. I love the memory of all three of them singing that song together.

So I turned my attention to him, as he was again concentrating on his toys spread out on the floor. I asked him what he liked best about school. He said, "My teacher." I asked him what he most liked to do in class, and he replied, "I like to read." I asked him what he does for fun, and he smiled when he said, "Take piano lessons." I then asked, "What do you want to be when you grow up?" Immediately he answered "I want to be a policeman and help a lot of people." Then, he looked up at me and said, "No, I changed my mind, I want to grow up and play the piano in my church."

I said, "Well, Tommy, I really think you can do both—be a policemen and play the piano in church." With that, he looked to the two women in that room to get their affirmation that, indeed, that really might be possible.

He went back to playing, and then suddenly stopped and looked up at me, taking his time to check out my white hair and wrinkles very carefully before asking (with all the innocence of a child), "What did you do before you got old?"

I thought for a minute and said, "When I was little like you, I wanted to grow up to be a mom. And when I grew up, I got to be a mom. So my dream came true." I asked him, "Do you think when you grow up that you can do what you really want to do?"

And he said, "I'm still little but I think so."

I finished this memorable dialogue between two people who had seventy years' difference in their age by saying, "If you believe hard enough, you can do anything." I then glanced at Jenny and Marilyn who had smiled their approval of the dialogue they had both heard between a little boy and an old woman.

As I left the parking lot of the Hospice Center shortly after that, I knew I needed to do something before I headed for home. I drove to our local book store and went to the children's section. There I found a copy of one of my most favorite books, which I have given to each of my grandchildren and my great-grandchildren. "The Little Engine That Could" had a powerful impact on me as a child—as it told me over and over again that, with hard work and determination, I could do anything. The lesson from that small book has as much power over me today as it did when I was six years old.

The next morning, I took the book to their room. I knew Tommy would be in school and found that Marilyn was in deep sleep. I asked Jenny if her daughter had a good night. She told me she wasn't awake much anymore. So, I gave Jenny the book I had bought for Tommy and asked her if she was familiar with it.

She brightened up and said, "I remember my own mother reading that to me, but I have forgotten all about it."

I asked if the next time Marilyn was awake, if Jenny would have her daughter sign the front of the book with something like, "To my beloved son, Tommy. You can do anything you set your mind to. I love you, Mom."

Toward the end of that week there was no more communication with the patient, but I visited with her mother, who always seemed grateful to see me. A few days later, life on this earth ended for Marilyn.

I had felt a special kind of closeness to Jenny and her mild manner of accepting life's challenges and making the most of them, which had obviously been passed on to her daughter and her grandson. So, since they lived in another town, she and I wrote notes to each other a couple of times. In one of those notes she told me that on the day of his mother's funeral, Tommy's father had drowned in a swimming accident.

Once in a while, when I am dusting the bookcase, I take out my favorite old book and say a prayer for that little boy. And, hopefully, he remembers—when he sees his mother's last note to him, written inside the cover of his book—that he can accomplish anything he wants with hard work and determination, even becoming a piano-playing policeman.

*Jesus loves me! This I know, For the Bible tells me so;*
*Little ones to Him belong; They are weak, but He is strong.*
*Yes, Jesus loves me! Yes, Jesus loves me! Yes, Jesus loves me!*
*The Bible tells me so.*
-- Public Domain

*I think I can.*
*I think I can.*
*I think I can.*
-- Watty Piper, 1930

*The person born with a talent they are meant to use*
*will find their greatest happiness in using it.*
-- Johann Wolfgang von Goethe

# Chapter Nineteen

## *Danny*

Upon entering the room in the Hospice Center, crowded with family members, I could see a young man, probably in his early thirty's, struggling for each breath.

The awkwardness when I entered the room was immediately palpable. I didn't know their names nor did they know mine.

The loved ones standing around him were not particularly fond of an unknown old white-haired woman quietly introducing herself as a Hospice volunteer. I greeted them by explaining my presence with the question, "In this private time with all of you gathered together, is there a special song that might give you comfort?"

No one answered. They either looked at each other or out the window. One man looked at the hymnal I always carry with me and asked, "Do you only sing church songs?" He looked at a couple of the others in the room and asked, "Do you know Danny Boy?"

Immediately I began to softly sing...

*Oh, Danny Boy, the pipes, the pipes are calling*
*From glen to glen, and down the mountain side,*
*The summer's gone, and all the roses falling.*
*It's you, it's you must go and I must bide.*

*But come ye back when summer's in the meadow,*
*Or when the valley's hushed and white with snow.*
*It's I'll be there in sunshine or in shadow,*
*Oh, Danny Boy, oh, Danny Boy, I love you so.*

Except for the sound of tears falling, the hush in the room was deafening. So, I very quietly said, "Our thoughts and prayers are with each of you. If we can help in any way, please let us know." And I slipped out of the room as quietly as I had entered.

As I walked down the hall, I heard someone coming up behind me. I turned, seeing it was the man who had requested the song. Through moist eyes, he smiled at me and said, "Thank you for that. It was exactly what all of us needed to hear because we didn't know how to say it to him. The young man you sang to is my son. His name is Danny and that has always been his favorite song."

*I said to Him, 'Here I am, Lord, send me.'*
-- Isaiah 6:8

*We were all given loving and compassionate attention*
*by family and even caring strangers*
*as we took our first few breaths*
*at the beginning of our lives.*

*The loving and compassionate attention*
*by family and caring Hospice personnel*
*assures us that the same is true*
*as we take our last few breaths*
*at the end of our lives.*
*-- JB*

# Chapter Twenty

## *Joe*

Once, maybe twice, we find ourselves in the role of being an involuntary volunteer.

Planning to give of your time and your compassion is one thing. Being in the right place at the right time in an unintentional exchange of a very brief, life-altering, and honest conversation, is something else altogether.

Such was the case with a neighbor and me. As soon as Joe and his wife moved in across the street, it was obvious that he was totally in control of everything, including her. It was quickly apparent that he was a bully due to a very mean spirit fed by out-of-control drinking. Over the course of five years, Noreen frantically and frequently called me on the phone to come quickly, usually because he had fallen in a drunken stupor. In one incident I saw blood all over the walls of the hallway, blood splattered over the food in the open pantry, and a knife on the table beside his chair. I found Noreen locked in an upstairs bedroom after having been hit by him. I called 911. After that, I refused to go over there when she called because I was admittedly afraid of him myself.

I always told her to call one of their two sons who lived nearby to come and help her, but they, too, were reluctant to be around their father because they were victims of his wrath as well.

The ambulance, police, and sheriff came from time to time until one hot summer day several years ago, when Joe was arrested for trying to kill Noreen in a fit of anger, and was led away in handcuffs to spend the next five months in jail. When he returned, he no longer drank, and was somewhat subdued by the multitude of medication that had become a large part of his daily routine.

However, his physical body had begun to deteriorate. He was showing the effects of his 83 years of hard living. And the last year of his life, he was in and out of the hospital more times than one could count. His diabetes was out of control, complicated by his latest diagnosis of lung cancer.

On a personal level, I always felt safe when Joe was in the hospital. If he would walk down his driveway at the same time I was walking down mine to get the mail, I would always wave and say, "Hi, Joe." Then I would quickly return to the safety of my home and close and lock the door behind me.

While I spent three or four days a week calling on my Hospice patients, as well as church members and friends, I deliberately avoided calling on Joe.

Then, one Sunday in church, I was reciting the Lord's Prayer, which I have done on a regular basis for over seven decades. All of a sudden, as I prayed, I tripped up on the words, "and forgive us our trespasses as we forgive those who trespass against us." I sat in the pew and asked myself what kind of Christian I was to give my compassion to strangers and friends, but not to Joe. And I realized that he, too, is a child of God.

In an absolutely spontaneous decision, I left the church immediately after the benediction and drove straight to the hospital. When I entered his room, he looked surprised as I smiled and greeted him. I walked to his bedside. He looked emaciated and very weak, and from my experience, I knew he was beginning the process of dying. I asked him how he was, and he said, "I am so tired." I said I knew he was and asked him if he had any appetite. He said no. I asked him if he wanted a drink of water, and he weakly said no. He then looked at me like he was expecting a lecture on how he needed to eat and drink.

The look of amazement when I said, "I know it is too much of an effort to do that, and it is ok if you don't," told me how grateful he was that I wasn't urging him to do so, like everyone else had been doing. Then he said, "I am worn out. I just want this to be over."

I said, "I know, and that's alright, too. It will be soon."

Again, he was relieved that I didn't give him a pep talk about unrealistic expectations of his recovery. Then he looked in my eyes and asked, in such a soft voice, "Judy, why are you always so happy?"

While he caught me off guard, I instantly answered, "Because I have found Heaven on earth in my everyday life, and I know that the joy of Heaven will be even greater."

He took a breath and, looking deep into my eyes, he said, "Tell me about Heaven."

Although those four words shocked me coming from a man who had truly frightened me for the past several years and who had physically and emotionally beat up every member of his family, I registered no surprise at the question as I calmly and softly answered, "Well, I don't know the specifics, but I am convinced that it is a place of overwhelming peace."

Then, with tears in his eyes, he looked up at me and said, "Judy, I have been a son of a bitch, and I know I won't get there."

Immediately, as I took his hand, I replied, "Yes, Joe, you truly have been. But that was in all of your yesterdays. This is today, and then it will be tomorrow."

With tears running down his cheeks, he said, "I may not be here tomorrow."

Again, I agreed with him (instead of placating him), saying, "No, Joe, you may not be."

He said, "Thank you for being honest with me."

And then, in that quiet, solemn moment, as peacefully I, too, was being relieved of my fear of him, I realized my next few words must be very simple, being careful not to use "religious" language. I continued, "If you want to find Heaven, what you have to do is very simple. When Noreen comes to visit you in a little while, take her hand in yours, and with all the sincerity of your soul, tell her that you love her deeply. And also, thank her for her loyalty and faithfulness to you for the past 59 years. Then when each of your children comes to see you, take their hand, look into their eyes, and tell them that you love them and also, thank them for staying with you through all the years. That's all you have to do. But don't say it if you don't mean it. It's all up to you."

I bent to kiss his forehead and said, "I'll see you again–either here or in Heaven, Joe."

And as I turned to leave the quiet of that hospital room, he uttered very weakly, "Wait, Judy, I love you, and thank you for being a friend to Noreen and me."

How I made it through the corridor, down the elevator, and across the parking lot, I don't know. The amazing gift of peace was filling that place in my soul where fear had lived for a long time. How humbled and blessed I was to be the person to give peace to a man who had stolen so much from so many.

Soon after that he was brought home to die. A few days later I went across the street to visit him in the hospital bed set up in their dining room. When I went to the bedside, he opened his eyes and said, "Hi, Judy".

"Hi, Joe," I replied, "Would you like me to sing a few hymns of comfort to you?"

He nodded ever so slightly as his eyes fell shut. For half an hour I softly sang hymns acknowledging his final journey down the path toward the Gates of Heaven. He lay there motionless, peacefully listening to the old words of those old hymns, which now had a new and very personal meaning...

*Just As I Am...thou wilt receive,*
*wilt welcome, pardon, cleanse, relieve...*

*Abide With Me....Heaven's morning breaks,*
*and earth's vain shadows flee;*
*...in life, in death, O Lord, abide with me.*

*Softly and tenderly Jesus is calling...*

*Amazing Grace..., 'tis grace hath brought me safe thus far,*
*and grace will lead me home.*

*Precious Lord, Take My Hand...*

I left, but within hours Noreen rushed to my front door. I met her as she said, "Please come quick, I think Joe is dying."

I put my arm around her as we walked across the street. When I got to his bedside, I took his hand and felt the last two pulse beats in his worn out body and soul, and then all was still. In the spirit of forgiven trespasses and love, I smiled and said to Noreen and their daughter, "He is finally at peace." Afterwards, Joe's two sons arrived as the darkness of night took over.

Since they didn't want me to leave, I stood quietly in the background as they each had their private moments. And then one of the sons, a large, very tall man came to me and folded me into his arms as he sobbed and said, "Thank you, Judy. Because of you, my dad told me that he loved me."

And very shortly after that, the other son came to me in the kitchen, his face wet with tears, and looked into my eyes as he hugged me tightly and said, "I was given the greatest gift I ever received the other day when Dad told me that he loved me and that he was proud of me."

His funeral was a service of celebration.

The blessing of being an involuntary volunteer at a most unexpected and unplanned time brings new meaning to the possibilities of experiencing compassion as deeply as those times when we plan our acts of the offering of ourselves for the comfort of others. The peace that passes all understanding is truly a gift to the giver as well as to the receiver. A gift of forgiveness, redemption, and love.

If ever there is a time when you truly want to volunteer, but seem to be held back because you are afraid you will say or do the wrong thing, take a very deep breath, letting go of your doubts, and say, with all the confidence in your being:

*Now go; I will help you speak*
*and will teach you what to say.*

This verse from Exodus 4:12 reminds us that in tending to the sick and lonely, we are never alone in offering comfort and compassion. Remember, God LEADS us—He doesn't leave us—when He calls us to be His hands and feet "to love one another."

-- JB

*In winter,*
*we yearn for the sunshine.*
*In life's last moments,*
*we yearn for the light of His Sonshine.*

*Dear Lord,*
*May I bring a glimmer of light so that, through the darkness,*
*one of your children may see the sunshine and feel the warmth*
*of your Sonshine. Amen.*
*-- JB*

# Chapter Twenty-One

## *Ruby*

As a hospice volunteer, there are some times when you simply sit quietly with your own thoughts and memories of the interaction you share with a particular patient. Whether you have known them for five days or five years, each person is special in their own way.

Such was the case with my patient, Ruby. She was 88 years old when I met her, and she was totally bed-bound. I never saw her sitting upright in the five years that followed. For five lovely years we were friends, appreciating the unusual length of time she lingered.

As I sat quietly in the church, waiting for her funeral to start, I kept looking at the open casket at the foot of the altar. She was finally at peace. In the corner of the coffin was the prayer shawl that I had made for her. She was never, ever without one of the four shawls I had made for her in our five years together. Not once, because she insisted that the nurses keep one over her shoulders at all times.

The organ music had stopped as the family and friends waited for the minister to begin the service. The funeral director walked down the aisle, and prepared to close the casket for the final time. He tucked in the satin sides, gently removed her glasses, and slipped them into his pocket, and with great tenderness, he took the prayer shawl, opened it, and covered her shoulders.

As volunteers, in whatever small way we share our time, our talents, and our gifts to those who need the gift of compassion and caring, the blessings we give, and the blessings we receive continue in life and in death.

I had been honored when Ruby's family asked me to give the eulogy at her funeral.

## EULOGY FOR RUBY

*I remember vividly the first minute I saw Ruby. Her family members, Diane and Stan, and Violet and Bob greeted me warmly in her room at the long-term care facility. Ruby did not look particularly happy that a stranger had entered her room early that Sunday afternoon.*

*When I again walked into her room at the nursing home a few days later, I had no idea of the lifelong depth of her shyness, and her uneasiness with strangers.*

*But, amazingly, we connected easily as friends because she was new to being totally dependent on others...and I was new to volunteering for our local hospice organization. She was only the second patient to whom I had been assigned.*

*As we became friends with each other, we quickly realized that we both shared a deep friendship with Jesus, as well. I went to see her at least two or three times every week for over five years. It became a routine, natural, and expected thing for me to sing her favorite hymn to her:*

*"What a Friend we have in Jesus*
*All our sins and griefs to bear.*
*What a privilege to carry*
*Everything to God in prayer.*
*Oh, what peace we often forfeit,*
*Oh, what needless pain we bear,*
*All because we do not carry*
*Everything to God in prayer."*

*We both knew how appropriate the words to that old hymn were for Ruby as she had lost her best friend, her husband of 62 years, just a few months before. Their marriage and their home had been deeply rooted in their love of their Lord.*

*As the months and years went on, I never failed to sing that hymn with every visit. Our friendship was so comfortable for both of us that I learned I could tease her. I doubt if many people could, or had, in the past. But, depending on how she was coping with her pain and discomfort, I would tease from time to time. I loved to see her blue eyes twinkle when she would point her finger at me and smile, as if to say "you got me again". On occasion, after we had chatted for a few minutes, I would pretend to leave without having sung "her" hymn. With the first step I would take toward the door of her small room, she would look at me sternly, and say very seriously, "You forgot something!" So, with both of us smiling at each other, I would sing "her" song while she "mouthed" the words right along with me.*

*We shared such happy conversations, fondly remembering the olden days when both of us were busy mothers and homemakers. We reminisced about how we would grow large gardens in the back yard and can countless quarts of vegetables to feed our families through the winter.*

*There was a period of time when she was somewhat disorientated and confused. Maybe it was just a part of the process of her very, very long journey, or maybe it was medication, but, one day, while in that state, I went to her bedside like I always did. I took her hand and smiled as I cheerfully said, "Hello there!", but there was no smile from her in return.*

*Instead, she looked at me for the longest time, and then, in her very soft voice, said, "I'm sorry. I don't remember your name, but I do remember that I love you." Oh my! What an affirmation that when Ruby loved you, you knew it.*

*There was never, ever any confusion, however, about how much she loved her family. Her memories of all of you were the most precious gift she had in every fiber of her life. Her devotion to each one of you, and your devotion to her, still fills this sanctuary today.*

*As I would point to a photo taped to the wall beside her bed in the nursing home, the stories she would tell were always filled with so much pride, so much love, and so much joy. Her body may have been frail, but her memories of her family were her strength.*

*We also shared such happy conversations about Heaven and the joyous reunion she would have with her beloved husband Larry, her grandson, her parents, and her many brothers and sisters. Since I had never, ever seen her upright, or out of bed, or seen her walk in all those years, we talked about the two of us meeting again someday. How we would hold hands and walk through the gardens of Heaven together, walking and talking and sharing more stories.*

*We always held hands. Through the years, Ruby held a lot of hands, the hands of her loyal and faithful children, the hands of her precious grandchildren.*

*As she entered the Gates of Heaven, it was fitting that she was holding the hand of her sister, Serena, when she took her last breath. Throughout her life, she always, always held Jesus' hand. Very appropriately, the last hymn I sang to her, an hour or so before she met her Jesus was "Precious Lord, take my hand".*

*And He did. Surrounded by love, and with the gift of peace, He took her hand…and led her home.*

Note: It is Ruby's hand I am holding on the cover of this book.

-- JB

*…and the hand of the Lord was with them.*

-- Acts 11:21

# Chapter Twenty-Two

## *Thomas*

Volunteering comes in many forms and at the most unexpected times.

After a particularly busy day, I had taken my shower early and gratefully put on my robe in anticipation of spending a couple hours just reading before bedtime.

The phone rang at 7:30 and the reply after I said "Hello" was "Will you go to the cemetery with me?" It was my neighbor who lived a couple of houses away who had recently been released from the hospital to continue her recuperation from pneumonia before facing a long and complicated surgery, to then be followed by months of rehabilitation.

She had been the full-time caregiver for her mother and her father for 22 years. Her mother had died a dozen years ago, and her father just one year ago. I had remembered the significance of this day, but Debra was never comfortable talking about "special" days.

So, when I heard that abrupt response to my answering the telephone, I knew that she, too, had been thinking of her dad's death a year ago today. Again she asked, "Will you go to the cemetery with me, and then get an ice cream cone afterwards?"

I covered my surprise and quickly said, "When?"

She answered just as quickly, "Now. I am sitting in your driveway!"

"Give me one minute to get dressed, and I'll be right out."

As we turned down the long lane into the cemetery in the slowly falling dusk of a rather cool summer evening, she said, "I haven't been out here since the funeral. Just haven't wanted to visit Dad and Mom here." Then she said, "Remember what you sang at the funeral home a year ago today and what you sang when we were standing under that tree over there?"

Having met Debra and her family at our church almost fifty years earlier, we had gone our separate ways and had no contact for the next four decades. With ease we had renewed our friendship and played cards and games three times a week with several other neighbors, who had all moved into our age-restricted neighborhood a few years ago. I had watched Thomas' declining health until he became wheelchair bound, and then became surrounded by the fog of dementia.

I had visited him often, both when he was in the hospital and then in the nursing homes many times in his last few years. He always called me by name even as his memory was fading. It became obvious that he would be entering the Gates of Heaven before long. One morning I went to see him in the hospital while two nurses were trying to get him to accept a treatment to aid his breathing, and he was unusually strong in his resistance!

He turned toward me and away from the nurses. They gave me thumbs up because I was distracting him.

I always carry a hymnal with me when I make my rounds visiting many nursing homes, the Hospice Center, and spend time with my own patients as a Hospice volunteer. So, while I had his attention, I said, "You know what, Thomas? I have never asked you in all these years to tell me what your favorite hymn is." He saw me flipping pages in my hymnal and again I asked, "Do you have a favorite hymn?"

He nodded yes. When I asked him what it was, he said in a steady, serious voice, "Let Me Call You Sweetheart." The nurses tried to stifle their giggle as I solemnly turned a few more pages until I "found" the one he requested and sang it to him.

And so, when I gave the eulogy at his funeral, we all joined in the singing of his favorite "hymn". There were lots of smiles amid the tears.

As Debra and I quietly got into the car and left the cemetery that night, she said, "Do you remember how much Dad loved it when I took him to get ice cream on those hot summer nights?"

In his honor, we sat for a long time at a table in his favorite restaurant, savoring a cup of ice cream. At one point both of us clinked our plastic cups together, and held them aloft in honor of a sweet man who had loved his family more than anything in his life.

It may have been an unusual one-year anniversary of the day Thomas entered Heaven, but it was an impromptu, unplanned celebration he would have loved.

*A friend loves at all times…*
-- Proverbs 17:17

*Thank you for the privilege we have
to serve You by serving others, Lord.*
-- JB

# Chapter Twenty-Three

## *Dominic*

One day I was visiting with a neighbor who was in the midst of trying to accept the challenges of aging. His latest surgery had not been successful and his ability to live independently was fading.

Very understandably, he was depressed as we talked. He talked, and I listened. Then he asked me a question and I talked. Somehow that irritated him even more because he wanted "magic" answers.

He blurted out, "There are times when you irritate me, Judy. Why don't things bother you? Why do you always act as if everything is going to be alright?"

He indicated that my being calm, my ability to expect a good solution to every challenge was a bad thing. He resented my patience. My peace was almost an insult to him in the upheaval and reality of the changes occurring rapidly in his life.

That was not the time or place to quietly tell him that *I have learned to be content in whatever state I am.* (Philippians 4:11) There is no greater blessing than to whisper that sentence as its meaning comes from the innermost corners of one's soul when life becomes a challenge.

So, I just smiled as I took his hand and said, "In whatever way I can express myself, dear friend, just know that I do hear your heart, and I do care."

Gratitude for the peace in my life simply overflows. I will not apologize for it. But my joy should not be an irritant to another person. May I be very, very aware to keep it contained at all times so as not to add pain to a hurting soul when my desire is to give comfort.

The challenge of sharing compassion, kindness, and understanding is sometimes not easy.

*Lord, make me an instrument of Thy Peace;*
*Where there is hatred, let me sow love;*
*Where there is injury, pardon;*
*Where there is error, truth;*
*Where there is doubt, faith;*
*Where there is despair, hope;*
*Where there is darkness, light;*
*And where there is sadness, joy.*

*O Divine Master,*
*Grant that I may not so much seek*
*To be consoled, as to console;*
*To be understood, as to understand;*
*To be loved as to love.*

*For it is in giving that we receive;*
*It is in pardoning that we are pardoned;*
*And it is in dying that we are born to eternal life. Amen.*
-- St. Francis of Assisi, 13th Century

# Chapter Twenty-Four

## *Abigail*

I had been a hospice volunteer for only a few months when one day the chaplain of one of our nursing homes stopped me in the hall and said, "I have heard you singing to your patients, and I have a favor to ask of you. Will you come with me to our Alzheimer's unit and sing to them?"

Already I had been assigned several patients and I was trying to make the best use of my time in order to visit with them as often as possible. I told her I wasn't sure about her request.

She said, "Well, will you come upstairs with me and sing to them just this once?"

I followed her up an elevator operated by a special code number and through a door at the end of the hall to which you also needed to use another code to enter. These were the most severely affected of the three units of people whose memories have left them and dementia has filled them.

She told me none of them had any conversational skills any more. As I looked around the room, I saw them seated in their wheelchairs at tables in their sunny gathering room. Most were sound asleep.

I quickly realized I needed to go into "monologue mode". So, I chatted for a few minutes and began to sing. I realized most of them were in a child-like state, so I started singing "Jingle Bells". (It was a lovely warm day in June). Two of them immediately opened their eyes and smiled! One even made "noises" which I interpreted as singing along. Encouraged, I sang, "You Are My Sunshine". A couple more eyes opened. Some didn't stay open very long. Some looked off in the distance, as if they might have heard that someplace, sometime before.

While the chaplain and the head nurse for that unit stood out in the hall watching, I started to sing a couple of hymns. No real reaction, but I already saw that in some far reaches of their minds, there might be a glimmer of a remembrance of days long gone.

I know that many times music can touch the soul when the spoken word cannot.

As I started to sing "Amazing Grace", I saw one rather large lady who was seated like a stone in her wheelchair. As I started the second verse, I noticed two dark spots on the royal blue tee shirt she was wearing. As I sang, the spots grew bigger. I realized the spots were falling tears. I continued singing as I pointed her out to the chaplain and nurse. They came in closer and saw that magical moment of recognition, as that lovely old hymn apparently touched a long forgotten memory in her diseased mind. The patient never opened her eyes. And the three of us couldn't see much, either, for the tears in ours.

When I finished that song, I told them I enjoyed spending time with them, and I walked out into the hall. The chaplain said, "Oh, Judy, won't you please come back?" I assured her that I would love to, but I didn't want to neglect the patients I had been given, and needed to be very judicious of my time. So once again, the chaplain said, "I will take any crumbs of leftover time you have."

I took a deep breath and said, "Sharon, I will be back next week." I sang to those lost souls every week for over five years.

# Chapter Twenty-Five

## *Lillian*

When I approached the door of a room in the Hospice Center, I noticed many family members standing around Lillian's bed, all holding hands. Immediately I realized they were praying, so I quietly stood there until they were finished.

With the last "Amen", several of them looked at me and smiled. And, since they had been praying, I knew they would find comfort in the singing of an old hymn. The family's pastor was among those eleven people in the group, and she introduced me to Lillian's husband who was sitting at the head of the bed, just inches from his wife's face. He acknowledged my presence as he held her hand. When I asked him if she had a favorite hymn, he said, "We have been praying and singing to her for the past 15 days, but she hasn't responded or even opened her eyes, so any hymn would be fine."

As I sang *In The Garden*, it was obvious to me that she would be taking Jesus' hand very soon. So, I began singing *Precious Lord, take my hand*.

And He did. As I sang the last few words of that hymn, she opened her eyes and looked into the weeping eyes of her husband. Then she closed her eyes again, took her last breath and lay in the stillness of her peaceful entry into Heaven as the last words of the hymn ended.

The eyes of her beloved family were on Lillian and her husband when he turned to me and said, "That was a miracle. Jesus is in this room." Their prayers had been answered in the stillness and beauty of the transition from her life on earth to her life in Heaven.

On that beautiful summer morning, a most comforting warmth brought the Sonshine into that room and calmly filled it with His perfect peace.

*Precious in the sight of the Lord is the death of His saints.*
-- Psalm 116:15

# Chapter Twenty-Six

## *Elise*

Not all volunteer experiences, even those involving calling on Hospice patients, are necessarily sad. Of course, the dying process is a very sobering experience, to always be treated with compassion and dignity. But a word or a phrase will bring a smile in expressing a death every once in a while.

Some folks are comfortable simply saying the phrase, "He died". Others say that someone "passed away", or simply "passed". Another phrase is, "She is now in Heaven", or "He just peacefully went to Heaven." In times long ago, the phrase, "She crossed over to the other side" was also used. And "He earned his final reward" was spoken frequently in generations gone by.

In my Hospice experience, I usually follow the lead of the family if, in fact, they use a certain phrase. But every once in a while I hear a new phrase.

Often times when I visit my patients in the nursing homes, I make friends with their roommates and their families, too. After several visits, both of the patients join me in conversation as they lie in their beds before I start to sing.

One morning I was going to visit my patient, Elise, and as I was walking down the hall to her room, the daughter of my patient's roommate was walking toward me. I could see that she was weeping, so

I figured out what must have happened to her mother.

When she saw me, she held out her arms for a hug. As I embraced her, she said, "Oh, Judy, my mama woke up dead this morning." Good thing I was hugging her when she said that because I was sure there was a slight smile on my face at that particular phrase!

I quickly reminded her of what she had told me a couple of weeks earlier when I had gone in to visit my own patient. The faithful daughter of the roommate was sitting beside her comatose mother, holding her hand and stroking her cheek. When I asked if either of them had a favorite hymn they wanted me to sing that day, the daughter said, "Sing a happy hymn because Mama is all done here on earth, and she is ready to dance into Heaven."

Quickly, I thought of exactly the right hymn, because of the look of comfort and peace on the face of the daughter as she heard:

*When we all get to Heaven,*
*What a day of rejoicing that will be.*
*When we all see Jesus,*
*We'll sing and dance the victory.*

When I left the room that morning, the director of the nursing home smiled as we passed each other in the hall. She said, "It sounded like you were having a party in there."

I hugged her and replied, "We were! We were just celebrating her arrival in Heaven a little early."

So there I stood, in the same hallway two weeks after singing that song, holding the grieving daughter in my arms. She finally took a deep breath and smiled as I looked into her tear-stained face and said, "She finally danced her 'happy dance'."

As Hospice volunteers, we are truly blessed to be a part of each end of life experience because, by whatever words we use, the result of a loved one no longer being in pain is the best gift.

*Rejoice in the Lord in all circumstances; again I say, 'Rejoice'.*
-- Philippians 4:4

# Chapter Twenty-Seven

## *Jean*

As I sat quietly by the bedside of one of God's children, who had celebrated over ninety birthdays here on earth, there was the warmth of peace in the silence. The only sound to fill the room was that of her shallow breathing.

Jean was one of my first patients to whom I had been assigned when I began my walk with Hospice. Our friendship grew with every visit, even though she was less than pleased when, as a stranger, I had walked toward her bed in the nursing home that first day. Our friendship quickly became a blessing, and I visited her two or three times a week. If she had the energy, we would chat and share memories of the olden days. Even though she was old enough to be my mother, I would join in the conversation, only to hear her say from time to time, "Oh, you're just a kid; you're only 74. Let me tell you how it really was."

Three years went by and her journey on earth was nearly complete. Her family had become real to me through her stories. Her husband was waiting for her in Heaven. We had talked often about the joyful reunion they would have when she joined him there.

For several weeks there had been no more conversation, but I knew she felt my presence as I would simply sit and hold her hand. Sometimes, I would softly sing her favorite old hymn. Sometimes, I would simply remind her that I loved her and that I knew she loved me too, as we had told each other so often in the past.

One cloudy day, I noticed how her thin well-worn wedding ring moved so easily on her finger whenever I would put her frail, bony hand in mine. How many times she had told me that plain band of metal was her most precious possession here on earth, and how it would become bright and shiny again when she and Herman would greet each other above.

I was humbled and honored to hold Jean's hand in the hours before she died, and to touch the old ring that had glowed for her on earth. New glow came to her in the quiet peace of death when Heaven became her new home...where Jesus and Herman were waiting.

*Give, and it will be given unto you.*
-- Luke 6:38

*In order to be the best volunteer I can be*
*I have learned that at times I must be still!*
-- JB

*Be still my soul...*
*...all safe and blessed, we shall meet at last.*
-- Katharina von Schlegal, 1752

# Chapter Twenty-Eight

## *Henry*

Henry was a handsome man in his late fifties. Even as he lay motionless in his bed in the Hospice Center, he was still handsome.

His wife, Helen, had sought me out some five years earlier when Henry had first been diagnosed with Alzheimer's. She was agonizing with the reality that she could no longer care for him at home and asked me many questions because she knew that I spend many hours each week with those special people.

She finally blurted out her real feelings, saying, "Judy, I can't do that to him. I can't put him in an extended care facility."

As I reached for her hand, I said, "Helen, you are giving him a huge gift, to let him share his long days surrounded with other people just like him. It will give him comfort to know, in the infrequent few moments when he does have the ability to think clearly, that he is not any 'different' than anyone else in that room. It will give him comfort to know that he is not a disappointment to you because he can't do what he used to do, or for him to see the sadness in your eyes that your beloved husband isn't the same man that you married. Nothing is expected of him, and that will be a relief for him. It will be your gift to him."

And now, five years later, she and I were sitting together in Henry's room at the Hospice Center. This was the seventh day that he had no food or water as per his wishes many years ago. Once again, she shared a different quandary with me. She said she would have him cremated, and then she would take his ashes to Pennsylvania to be buried next to his folks. She, too, would be buried there some day.

Then her face clouded over and she said, "But, Judy, I don't know what to do now, right now. This part of the journey is so blurred. I have dealt with the Alzheimer's, and I am comforted with the burial in our home town, but I do not want a funeral in the church. I don't want all those kind people coming up to me and telling me how sorry they are, and I don't want to just stand beside a picture of Henry at the funeral home, with those same people saying the same thing. I know they are sorry. I have heard that for the past five years, but I know I need some kind of closure."

So, while the two of us were sitting next to his bed talking, I said, "Helen, why don't you have a private funeral right here in this very room with you and your sons a few minutes after Henry takes his last breath?"

"Can I do that?"

"Yes", I replied. "You will be the most important person in this room at that time, and you can do whatever makes you comfortable."

She was stroking Henry's arm at the time, and she said to him, "Do you hear that, honey? You always told me that I was the most important person in your world."

Since we attend the same church, we both knew that our Pastor of Visitation, who had been faithfully calling on both of them through the years, would be going on a two week vacation in a couple of days. So she said, "If the pastor isn't here when Henry dies, do I have to have a clergyman officiate the funeral?"

I answered that a funeral is a service to comfort the living, so she could do whatever gives her peace.

She then said, "So, if the minister isn't here, will you do it, Judy?"

I answered that I would be honored to do that for both her and Henry, and that the hospice chaplain would be glad to help, too.

Late that afternoon, when I was getting ready to leave, I told Helen to call me at any hour of the night, because I could be at the Hospice Center in five minutes, and she seemed relieved. She had told me that their sons were going to arrive from the airport around supper time, so they would talk about the conversation we had earlier.

The next morning I could see a marked difference in how labored Henry's breathing had become. I knew his life of confusion here on earth was about to end. Helen was surrounded by two of her sons, as the third son was unable to get there from Oregon, but was with them via the speaker on their cell phone. Around noon the long good-bye was over. We all formed a circle around the bed as Helen held one of Henry's hands, and one of the sons held his other hand. And after a prayer, a scripture verse, and three of their favorite hymns, the celebratory service of Henry's release into his new life had taken place. As we hugged, Helen smiled and said, "It was perfect."

*When God's children are in need,*
*you be the one to help them out.*
-- Romans 12:13

*There is a place of full release, near to the heart of God;*
*A place where all is joy and peace, near to the heart of God.*
*O Jesus, blest Redeemer, sent from the heart of God,*
*hold us who wait before Thee near to the heart of God.*
-- Cleland B. McAfee, 1903

# Chapter Twenty-Nine

## *Alice*

And then there is Alice, an 84-year old Alzheimer's patient whom I have visited for several years.

As her dementia has increased, her sense of "time" has decreased. She no longer remembers whether I visit her every day or a couple of times a week. Over the past several months, I am more likely to find her very deep in sleep, so she hasn't always been aware of my presence. But, that does not discourage me because I know I am in her presence, sharing a totally silent visit. In those times, I can feel her peace, a gift given to those who are fading in the fog of that insidious disease.

The other day I was delighted to find her awake as she sat comfortably in her recliner, snuggled under her favorite pink blanket. Even better, she smiled sweetly when her eyes finally opened, and she focused enough on me to hold out her hand for me to take. What a gift that is for me and her loving family on the rare occasion when this happens.

I happily squeezed her thin hand ever so slightly and said, "I am so glad to see your smiling blue eyes. You look so cozy under your pretty blanket. It must be nice and warm, too, because I know your favorite color is pink."

She looked so surprised as she asked, "How do you know that?"

"Because you told me what your favorite color was a long time ago."

"Oh", then she asked, "Are we new friends or old friends?"

Quickly I answered, "We are good friends."

She simply responded, "That's nice". Her eyes then closed in her weariness of holding them open, and she once again, drifted off into the special place in which she finds her peaceful existence now.

That was the beginning and the end of another blessed visit, but it filled me with gratitude, once again, at being led to my life of volunteering.

*Serve one another humbly in love.*
-- Galatians 5:13

*As a Hospice volunteer, I don't hesitate to make friends with my patients. I realize that, as new friends, we may not become old friends. I simply embrace the fact that we are "today" friends.*
-- JB

# Chapter Thirty

## *Agatha*

We can volunteer our care and compassion for others in some of the most unexpected ways. And because of these unplanned encounters, lives can be blessed even in the hustle and bustle of plodding through an ordinary day.

Some of our best blessings during the waking hours of any day are the interruptions that we bump into along the way. They can even be a mistake. I learned early on that you don't have to be a trained volunteer or an experienced counselor to bring a ray of sunshine to a stranger.

Most of my working life was spent in telephone sales. I can hardly recall the variety of all those jobs. I sold ads for yellow pages for the telephone company. I sold magazine subscriptions. I made appointments for aluminum siding salesmen and insurance men. I worked for thirty years for a food company, calling my almost 1700 customers on a regular basis. The size of my paycheck depended solely on my efficiency and discipline. No perks, no retirement plan, nothing except my ability to do my job. Those jobs taught me that success always depends a great deal on the enthusiasm you bring to your job, whatever it is. Enthusiasm and also gratitude.

One bright, sunshiny morning I dialed the number of an out-of-town customer, and when an elderly voice answered, I asked, cheerfully, "Mary Ellen?"

"Who?"

"Mary Ellen?" I repeated.

"Who is this?"

"Judy with (name of company). Is Mary Ellen there?"

"Nobody named Mary Ellen here, honey. My name is Agatha, but I'll talk to you."

"Oh, I'm, sorry. I must have dialed the wrong number", I replied.

"That's ok, honey, you got me at my number. Ain't nobody never calls me, so we can talk. What is your name again?"

I hesitated, then told her again, and she went right on talking as if I hadn't even answered.

"I live here all alone, and it always startles me when my phone rings, 'cuz I ain't got no kin and only this telephone 'case I have an emergency. I lives way out here in my little place and, 'septin' for the mail lady, I just talk to my cats."

As I looked at the long list of names I needed to call before I stopped for lunch, I just kept on listening, until finally she stopped and said, "Honey, do you live around here? If so, you'd be welcome to come see me."

As I chuckled, I told her that I lived in another state and that my job is to call my customers all day long. She had trouble understanding that I could afford to call people in another state. So I tried to explain that I had a WATS line in my home, and the company I worked for paid for the phone, as long as I would sell their product.

So she said, "Oh, do you want me to buy something? What do you sell?"

I told her that I sold food products and assured her that I didn't call to sell her something. In fact, I had just dialed her number by mistake, adding that while I had enjoyed chatting with her, I was again sorry to have bothered her.

Immediately she went right on, with our mostly one-sided conversation, and since I had mentioned food, she began telling me about the old family recipes she had used that had been in her family of farmers for generations. She emphasized that this younger generation was going to be sorry they ate these foods that come out of a box. Even more appalling to her was the fact that some folks, even young parents with little children, now pull up to a restaurant and don't even get out of the car because someone passes them a meal in a sack that they eat in the car. "Can you imagine that?" she asked.

On and on she went, as I smiled to myself at her perceptions of this "modern world". All I had said was that I worked for a food company. Ten more minutes passed while I relaxed in my chair and listened to her joy at having someone to talk to.

Then, as if she remembered how we had "met", she suddenly said, "Will you call me again tomorrow?"

I quickly laughed and said, "Well, I can't do that because I don't even know your phone number."

She didn't say anything for several seconds, and then asked me, "But how did you call me if you didn't know my number?"

Explaining that I had dialed a wrong number, she sounded so forlorn as she said to me in such a quiet voice, "Oh, then I guess you'll never call me again."

And as I took my next breath, I said, "If you give me your phone number, I will call you again someday because you have made me smile this morning."

Again there was silence as she tried to process the fact that I had called her about fifteen minutes before, but I didn't even know her number.

So, as cheerfully as I could, I said, "Oh, wasn't this a 'happy mistake' that I made when I punched the wrong number on my phone? So if you tell me what the right number is to get a hold of you, I will call you another time, and we can chat again."

She did. And I did, several times.

Then, one day, as I waited for her to answer, I got a recording that said, "The number you have dialed is no longer a working number."

With a bit of sadness, I hung up, looked out the window into the distance, and thanked God that what we consider a mistake or an interruption is often an unexpected moment of joy that brightens our lives, and also the lives of someone we have never even met.

*Each of you should give what you have decided in your heart to give,*
*not reluctantly or under compulsion, for God loves a cheerful giver.*
-- Corinthians 9:7-9

*We make a living by what we get,*
*we make a life by what we give.*
-- Winston Churchill

# Chapter Thirty-One

## *Benjamin*

When I first met Benjamin, there was little communication between us. It wasn't that he was particularly unfriendly, but I quickly learned that he had little "life experience", which caused him to be a bit timid.

He was 82 years old when he became my patient, and I found out that he had been a farmer all his life. Having never married, he had managed to live alone for decades in the farmhouse that had been his parents' home. For years he had been totally wheelchair-bound.

Benjamin was a pleasant man of few words. One time he asked me if I knew most of the songs in "that book", since I carry my hymnal with me every time I leave home. It was then that he told me his favorite hymn was "The Old Rugged Cross". So, our future conversations eased into comfortable chats of weather, soil conditions, and farming, along with his memories of when he was physically able to go to church. And with most visits, his question was, "Are you thinking of singing something today?"

One day he was noticeably very ill as he lay quietly in his bed. When I entered his quiet room on that dreary, gray winter afternoon, he was looking longingly out the window. Immediately, he began the conversation, almost as if he had been waiting for me, saying, "Can we talk about Heaven today? You are the only person I know who is comfortable having a conversation about Heaven."

He laughed when I said, "I would love to, but you do realize that I don't talk about it from experience because I haven't been there. I love the thought of going there some day."

He smiled and said, "Me, too, I can hardly wait to get there, but have never said that to anybody. Oh, I guess I have never said that to myself, either."

He looked longingly out the window again and then asked, "Will there be snow in Heaven? I love it when Jesus covers our whole world with white. And then the snow melts and I can see the ground. I always knew that if I was patient, the white would disappear into the brown, but finally the green would come." (Ever the farmer, he was lost in the seasons of God's world around us.) Again he turned to me and asked, "Will there be rain in Heaven?"

I laughed and said, "Well, Benjamin, I can't say first hand, but wouldn't there have to be rain in Heaven in order to have the endless gardens of flowers?"

He added, "And the fields of corn and beans?" (Once a farmer, always a farmer.)

So, I said, "Hey, I never thought of this before, but I wouldn't be surprised if there are even tractors in Heaven", to which he laughed out loud, in the midst of his pain.

Talking had been kind of an effort for him, so I asked him if I could sing some hymns while we were thinking about the beauty of Heaven. After sharing "For The Beauty of the Earth", "This Is My Father's World", and "In The Garden", I finished with…"Turn Your Eyes Upon Jesus".

Since he was getting tired, I said a prayer, thanking God for the ease at which the two of us could talk about the Heaven that we will be glad to see in person one day. As I was driving home, I also thanked God for giving me the peace to be able to share unplanned conversations with those who desperately need to talk to someone who is willing to listen to them. Strangers when we met, but in time, we became comfortable friends on the same journey.

# Chapter Thirty-Two

## *Bertha*

One morning I was singing to a patient who was sitting in her wheelchair along the wall in the hallway of a nursing home. There were many others all lined up, one behind the other all down the corridor.

Bertha would join in singing a few lines from some of the hymns from time to time, but I knew she just loved them all, so I went from one to the other. Then, I realized she had been still for a little while. Her eyes were closed all the time, since she was blind.

So I quietly asked, "Are you asleep?"

In a couple of nano-seconds I heard, "Yes!"

I laughed right out loud, as did a couple of aides at the nurses' station beside where her chair had been parked.

And then, the patient also laughed out loud as she replayed the question and answer in her mind!

I bent down and hugged her and said, "I'm so glad I came to see you today. It might be dreary and rainy outside, but you brought the sunshine in here this afternoon."

*All people that on earth do dwell,*
*Sing to the Lord with cheerful voice,*
*Him serve with mirth, his praise forth tell,*
*Come ye before him and rejoice.*
-- William Kethe, 1561

*…my cup of blessings overflows.*
-- Psalm 23:5

*Volunteering is not a singular act.*
*It may be a blessing to give kindness or compassion to a friend or a stranger.*
*But, oh, the gift of fulfillment received by those who volunteer is truly a "reversed*
*blessing" felt by the giver which warms the souls of both with gratitude.*
-- JB

# Chapter Thirty-Three

## *Joseph*

It was the Sunday before Memorial Day. In our church, the tradition is for the congregation to sing three or four patriotic songs before the service begins.

However, for whatever reason, there was no singing of those beloved old songs that morning, and several in the congregation looked puzzled. As the service went on, the pastor didn't mention the remembrance of this holiday as he was focusing on its being Pentecost Sunday, and the meaning of that special day in the history of the church.

After the service ended, I was chatting with several friends in our Fellowship Hall when I learned that our former pastor had been taken to the hospital the day before. I had known him for over 50 years and had visited with him several times a week since he had been admitted to a nursing home after he had fallen several months earlier. So I left church and went immediately to the hospital.

When I entered his room, shortly afterwards, Joseph was lying there wide awake in the silence of a hospital on a Sunday morning in the middle of a holiday weekend. His 96-year-old face brightened up as he recognized me. His sons live out of town, but I was still surprised that his room was empty of visitors because he is a very highly regarded man, having spent decades in the service of our country as well as decades as a minister in the service of our Lord.

He is the kind of man who commands the attention of any room in which he enters. He was a creature of habit, including sitting in the same pew at the second service at our church every single Sunday after he retired. The seat on the aisle half way down the Sanctuary is known as "Joseph's pew". Since I go to the first service, I sit in that seat. He loves it when I go into his nursing home room and teasingly say, "Hey, Joseph, I sat in your seat last Sunday."

So, as we chatted and I found out he was still undergoing tests and observation, I realized that, from time to time, he was disoriented, thinking he was still in his bed in the nursing home.

Then suddenly he took command of the conversation and said, "Tell me about the sermon this morning. Did the minister praise the veterans?"

Well, in the interest of truth, I answered that he hadn't.

"Cynthia and I always looked forward to being able to sing those patriotic songs out loud in the church on this day every year." He went on, "Those hymns are in our hymnal, you know. You did sing them beforehand so that those in the congregation who served were reminded in song about the glory of our Country, didn't you?"

"Well, no, we didn't," I had to answer.

Immediately I said, 'Hey, Joseph, both you and I missed singing them this morning, so let's do it right now, right here." He reached out and took my hand as I started singing "God Bless America". He joined me in his weak bass voice as he looked off in space. I knew his mind was going back decades to some battlefield someplace overseas.

When we got to the phrase, "…my home, sweet home", he then raised his other hand, closed his eyes, and pointed to Heaven. Oh my! How powerful and meaningful to be alone with him at that time and in that place, beside the hospital bed of a man who had been given, among his many, many awards, the Quilt of Valor several months earlier. To be singing that song with this highly decorated former chaplain and officer of the US Navy was a most humble, yet meaningful, blessing.

When we were done, I bent over and kissed his forehead and thanked him for all he has done for all of us. And I also reminded him of all the ways God has blessed so many of us, through his ministry after he returned home from the service.

As I was slowly walking through the hospital parking lot, I realized I had just participated in a most meaningful Memorial Day service, and there were only two people in attendance.

*Precious in the sight of the Lord is the death of His faithful servants.*
-- Psalm 116:15

*Christ has no body now on earth but yours;*
*yours are the only hands with which He can do His work,*
*yours are the only feet with which He can go about the world,*
*yours are the only eyes through which His compassion can shine forth...*
-- St. Teresa of Avila

# Chapter Thirty-Four

## *Stanley*

Yesterday I was standing in front of the spice aisle at the store, somewhere between basil and oregano, simply trying to find a tin of cinnamon.

I was interrupted in my total concentration by a voice behind me that said, "Excuse me, are you the Singing Lady?"

As I turned, I had no idea who this man was as I smiled and stammered, "Well, yes, I do answer to that name." Puzzled, I then added, "I am so sorry, but I am not sure I know you."

He then smiled and wistfully said, "Oh, we have never met, even though I have seen you a few times. Several months ago my wife was the roommate of one of your hospice patients in the nursing home. There was a curtain separating the two of them. But whenever you would sing to your patient, my wife would close her eyes and just listen, too."

As he looked off in space, he added, "Several times I would go to visit her and ask her how she was that day. And she would smile and say, "I'm doing better today because the Singing Lady was here." My wife is no longer here, but I know she would want me to thank you."

He then pushed his cart on down the aisle, and as I stood there overwhelmed by the feeling of being blessed at the most unexpected times and in the most unexpected places once again, I was renewed once again by the gift of being a volunteer.

*Where he leads me, I will follow…*
*Where he leads me, I will follow…*
*Where he leads me, I will follow…*
*I'll go with him, with him all the way.*
-- E.W. Blandy, 1890

*The Lord has told you what He wants from you:*
*to be fair and just and merciful, and to walk humbly with your God.*
-- Micah 6:8

*Volunteering*
*makes my heart smile.*
-- JB

# Chapter Thirty-Five

## *Barbara*

For almost four years, Barbara has been in the memory care unit of one of the retirement communities where I sing every Friday morning. As I enter the dining area of these special people who live in the constant fog of Alzheimer's disease, Barbara would nearly always recognize me and smile her shy smile as I stood among the group and sang simple songs of old while they ate their breakfast.

Most times, she would join in with favorites like "Let Me Call You Sweetheart", "Down By The Old Mill Stream", and "Amazing Grace". She loved it when we sang, "If You're Happy and You Know It, Clap Your Hands", and she would clap at the appropriate time.

I never heard her speak but I saw her sing along, always accompanied by a smile.

She had not been at her usual seat on that particular Friday morning, but I didn't think anything of it, dismissing her absence as thinking she probably was sleeping late.

As is my custom, I drive to three or four more facilities in town, singing to my individual patients, as well as to gathered groups in several nursing homes, and a couple of private homes which house six residents each.

When I walked into the physical therapy room of our newest nursing home, I was greeted, as always, with lots of smiles from the staff as well as some of the residents who were trying to regain the use of their arms or legs as they worked the machines.

However, I noticed a cluster of three therapists trying to get the attention of someone who was slumped down in a wheelchair facing away from me. As the group requested certain songs, I was somehow drawn to wander over to that corner of the room. As I walked closer, I discovered the motionless woman in the wheelchair was Barbara!

I bent down so she could see me, but she kept her face turned toward the wall. I quietly said, "Barbara, it's Judy," but she didn't move. I realized the look in her eyes was fear. Very gently, I cupped her chin in my hand and turned her face to me. Again, I softly said, "Hey, Sweetheart, it's me, it's Judy."

Seeing my royal blue Hospice jacket and the hymnal I always carry, along with my white hair that says, "We all have our age in common . . .", she finally, very slowly turned toward me. When she made eye contact with me, my heart melted, because I knew that she knew me. For someone suffering from dementia, any change of scenery or people fills them with immobilizing fear.

One time a patient's family moved a picture on the wall at the foot of her bed to another wall, and she became uncontrollably agitated. The staff increased her medication to no avail. A few days later, I wandered in to visit with her, and, as always, when I would sing, "Cruisin' Down The River", I would point to the picture of Barbara and her husband in their boat from days long ago. Since it wasn't in its usual place, I innocently took the picture off the wall and handed it to Barbara while I sang. She quieted down remarkably. When I left, I put it back in the old place where it had hung at the foot of her bed. Amazingly, she became docile enough that the extra medication was no longer necessary.

Patients with memory problems do not like anything in their small confused world changed. Early on in my visitations, I had learned this, and Barbara just validated it. That is why I never, ever make a call without wearing my familiar jacket. Additionally, when I counsel family members who say that their mother doesn't recognize them anymore, I tell them to pick out a favorite shirt or blouse and wear it every single time they go to visit. The familiarity of sameness really does seem to help in some cases.

At any rate, as I still held Barbara's chin in my hand, I gently repeated, 'Hello. It is Friday morning and I came to see you. And I need you to help me sing." As I still stayed close to her face, blocking out everyone and everything around her, I started to sing "Jesus Loves Me", and miraculously, she joined in, singing very softly out loud. Immediately, I went right on to sing, "You Are My Sunshine", and again, she joined in ever so softly.

I could see tears running down the cheeks of all three staff members as they sat right there in our little corner of the world, watching the small miracle of a soul emerge from the depths of the unknown to the surroundings of comfort.

*Since you have been chosen by God who has given you this new kind of life, and because of his deep love and concern for you, you should practice tenderhearted mercy and kindness to others.*
-- Colossians 3:12

*The best love of all is that which you give away.*
-- JB

# Chapter Thirty-Six

## *Art*

When we volunteer, we don't always know how our one act of kindness or compassion will affect someone else.

One day I took a prayer shawl with me when I went to see Art, a very ill man in the Hospice Center. The patient's brother, an active member of my church, was in the room, too. As he greeted me warmly with a hug, Jerry asked me, "Are you going to sing something to my brother again today? He seems to be getting weaker."

"Yes", I answered, but added, "Before I do, I thought you might like this prayer shawl to warm you as you spend so many hours sitting here beside your brother."

Several days after the funeral, I received this note from Jerry: "As my brother lay dying, I placed the prayer shawl on his chest and, like a net, it caught his last breath. It is now my most treasured possession."

In volunteering, the blessings of the one who gives and the one who receives are truly intermingled.

*Breathe on me, Breath of God,*
*fill me with life anew,*
*that I may love what thou dost love,*
*and do what thou wouldst do.*

*Breathe on me, Breath of God,*
*so shall I never die,*
*but live with thee the perfect life*
*of thine eternity.*
-- Edwin Hatch 1878

*If I speak in the tongues of men or of angels, but do not have love,*
*I am only a resounding gong or a clanging cymbal.*
-- I Corinthians 13:1

*Our lives are to be used and, thus, to be lived as fully as possible. And truly it*
*seems we are never so alive as when we concern ourselves with other people.*
-- Harry Chapin

# Epilogue

## *Random Thoughts*

### AFTER THE DEATH OF A LOVED ONE

There is never an easy time to say your final good-bye to a loved one. Those first special days – birthdays, Christmas, anniversaries – can be difficult. No one is immune to the emotional upheaval in the remembrance of days of importance in the first year or two after a death. However, the sudden appearance of tears of loneliness at unexpected times, sometimes many years later, can also blindside you.

The first December can be difficult as traditions of many years of memories almost assault your senses with the sights and smells and sounds of joy, which seem to suffocate you at times. Your family gathers together, but the emptiness crowds the room. Sometimes you embrace the kind and loving people around you. And at other times, you want to retreat to your own private space as your emotions consume you.

### BE PATIENT WITH YOURSELF

Remember that long, long ago shepherds in the fields watched intently over every single sheep. The Wise Men watched a very special star. They watched and waited. And when the time was right, they then followed that unknown path.

So, the first Christmas season without your loved one, you, like the shepherds and wise men of old, may also be filled with a watching and waiting to be led onto your new unknown path ahead.

## BE KIND TO YOURSELF

Let the cleansing tears of sadness flow. Your sorrow is truly not forgotten by others. And it is surely not forgotten by God. He will continue to hold your hand. Isaiah 55:12 says, "You will find joy and be led forth in peace!"

As it was long, long ago, Silent Night will be followed by Joy To The World.

Special days can be challenging. Something as ordinary as ironing, eating lunch, or baking brownies can trigger unexpected emotions.

One December day, a neighbor called me. It had been five months since her husband had died. Lynn and Dale had a very loving and attentive family and after his stroke, they all walked his last journey together.

So when my phone rang, Lynn said, "I think I just heard Dale laugh at me."

She went on to say that she always used to iron Dale's handkerchiefs. And he always laughed at her, telling her how ridiculous that was. She then added that after years of his using his handkerchiefs also as paint rags and for wiping up spilled oil, she quit ironing them.

Well, a few days before Christmas one of her daughters called and asked her mom if she still had her dad's old handkerchiefs. Lynn said that she did. The daughter then told her that she had found an old picture of her dad sitting in his boat with a big grin on his face, and so she had made copies to give to several family members as a Christmas gift in a few days. She told my friend that she wanted to use her dad's handkerchiefs to wrap each frame! She said, "I know everyone will cry when they see Dad's picture, so this way they'll be prepared."

Just before we hung up, Lynn added, "You were right, I found the tears running down my cheeks as I was ironing, because I knew Dale was laughing at me for pressing his handkerchiefs one last time. We sure never know when those memories will turn on the water works, but today my tears were both of joy as well as sadness. Not only are we all going to miss him desperately all over again in a few days, but we will also be filled with joy that we have the simple memories of the happy times we spent together."

Right after the funeral of my own daughter, who died at the age of 49, I had a well-developed young tree planted right outside my dining room/kitchen window. On the day of my Jannie's first birthday in Heaven, I was pleased that I was getting through that special day pretty well. It was mid-October and the leaves on the trees were turning lovely shades of yellow and gold, orange and red. The windows were open as I was eating my lunch, thinking that when I was done, I should go outside and transplant some tulip bulbs to a better place for next Spring's flowering.

For some unknown reason, ever since she was a little girl, I had always called Jannie my chickadee. All of a sudden, out of the corner of my eye, I saw a flash. Looking up, I saw that a lone chickadee had perched on the closest limb to the window and was looking right in at me as it began to sing. When that ordinary peaceful sight and sound broke the quiet of a plain mid-day lunch, I dissolved into a puddle of tears.

In these moments that visit all of us so unexpectedly, after we compose ourselves once again, we need to remember that the memories of our hearts are truly gifts to treasure. How sad to be devoid of memories of days spent with loved ones. Through tears, may we sharpen our sense of gratitude for what was, and for the knowledge that, while those were the best of days, the simple singing of the birds will lead us on.

One day I saw a friend with whom I had sat every day in the quiet peace of a Hospice room for the last thirteen days of her beloved husband's earthly life. After we exchanged a meaningful hug, she looked in my eyes and said, "You were right. I have been doing pretty well until, out of the blue, I was totally blindsided and ended up crying for several hours. It was over the silliest thing, too."

As we sat down to continue our chat, she went on, "Whenever I made brownies, I always made sure I prepared them when Jeff was about to come home from work. He said that was his 'job' to scrape any remaining mixture from the sides of the bowl with the big spoon before I put the pan in the oven." And, together, they always enjoyed a warm brownie even if it was right before a meal.

She then said, "All was going well the other day until, without thinking, I had put the mixing bowl of brownie batter on the same spot on the counter in the kitchen where I had always left it for him."

I asked her if she had cleaned out the bowl with the big spoon the other day, and she answered with a big, "Nope."

I then asked her if she ate a brownie when it was warm out of the oven, and again she said, "Nope."

So I asked her if she eventually ate the brownies, and it was then that her eyes twinkled again as she answered, "Well, he wouldn't have wanted me to waste them!"

In whatever way, at whatever time, for however long it takes, when a memory sneaks up on you, often accompanied by tears, remember the blessing that caused those tears. The blessing of memories. The gift of memories. Your loved one would be the first one to say:

Be kind to yourself!
Be patient with yourself.
JB

## PRAYER FOR FAMILY OF HOSPICE PATIENT

May our precious Lord gift you with the warmth of His peace in the next few hours, days, and weeks as you walk through the challenge of your new now.

May our precious Lord gift you with serenity in the beautiful memories you share from the past as well as in the future memories of love and compassion which are being offered by others now. May you accept acts of kindness and concern from others in the spirit of caring in which they are offered, allowing others to be blessed by blessing you.

May our precious Lord gift you with the reassurance of His Presence as He holds your hand on this journey. In His loving plan to welcome your loved one into the Gates of Heaven, believe anew that He will replace all weariness and pain with the peace which passes all understanding. Amen. -- JB

## VOLUNTEERING

While the emphasis of this book has been the one-to-one visitation of the sick and lonely, the ways to volunteer are endless. In fact, the largest majority of volunteering is not in individual visitation. However, the purpose of the examples given in this book are to emphasize the blessings of the giving as well as the receiving of kindness and compassion from just one person. The gift of volunteering in an organized group or charity is absolutely every bit as important as the giving of your time and your talent individually.

Dedicating your act of caring and support, financially, physically, or spiritually in any capacity is truly a dedication in the highest form of service. "Love one another" can be demonstrated in a multitude of ways. You don't have to be a worshipper of a certain religion to experience the special feeling that fills you when you lose yourself in giving a part of yourself to helping others. The spontaneous act of kindness to a stranger can oftentimes affect you more than the person whom you assisted for a fleeting moment in time.

By whatever method you may choose to volunteer, the "getting started" step is often the hardest step to take.

I liken this to an article written by Lisa Bevere that I read in "A Gentle Spirit" a long time ago. It reads as follows:

> *We often find ourselves surrounded by the unfamiliar and unfriendly. God wakes us up from the secure by pushing us out of our comfort zone. By comfort zone, I am referring to all that is familiar, expected, constant, and under our own control.*
>
> *God is more concerned with our condition than with our comfort. At times He stirs our nests to make our comforting things uncomfortable.*
>
> *This is how young eagles get their flight training. The mother eagle grabs the nest with her talons and flaps her wings up and down, blowing all the nice, comfortable padding out of the nest. She tears up what she had so carefully provided. Then she takes each baby eagle and carries it outside of the nest into the wind. This is where young eagles learn to fly. They can't try their wings if they are sitting in the nest.*

And so it is with volunteering. You can't discover the joy of being a volunteer if you are sitting in your nest.

## SUGGESTIONS FOR VOLUNTEERING

How often I have heard someone say, "I couldn't do what you do. I don't sing." Or, "I am not comfortable in a nursing home because it is too depressing." Or, "I am the world's worst cook, so I can't take food to someone." I have also heard, "I don't know what to say to someone who is hurting or sad." Or, "I don't want to call someone on the phone because I might bother them."

The excuses not to volunteer are many, and they are valid ones. But, there are ways to give of your time, your talent, and your compassion that will fit anyone who simply has the desire to bring a smile to someone else. To remind them that they matter to you.

If your comfort level is not working with someone in need one on one, there are many, many organizations and charities where groups work together toward a common goal. Call the United Way in your town to see how you can help. Offer your help to any group who runs a day care for the young or the elderly. Be a mentor to an agency whose objective is to help children with after school care. Hospitals always need volunteers. There are many ways to assist in a church or synagogue.

Individually, there are endless ways to volunteer. If you can't talk comfortably with a person who is ill, if your physical ability is limited, or if your time is too involved with everyday life, you can still show your concern. Send a note or card to someone who is ill or lonely, telling them that you are thinking of them. You can send a gas card anonymously to someone who does volunteer work, thanking them for what they do for others.

Don't let your hesitancy in knowing what to say in a conversation stop you from showing an unexpected act of kindness. Flowers are always appropriate. Of course, they could be delivered by your local flower shop. Or, when you go to the grocery store, pick up a small bouquet and drop it off to someone who is lonely or elderly or not feeling well. If conversation is difficult for you, just say you are on your way home and need to put your groceries away, but wanted them to know you have been thinking of them.

The normal journey of aging comes with many challenges:

- Mobility issues, unsteady on their feet.
- Financial problems
- No longer able to drive
- Unable to do chores (scrub floors, wash windows, lawn care, etc.)
- Nutritional deficiency due to sadness of eating alone or inability to get food
- Very little socialization
- Not wishing to be a bother to someone else
- Feelings of being an obligation instead of a choice to family and friends

However, the list of solutions to the problems is much longer than the list of problems, such as:

- Call someone who lives alone and say you were just thinking of them.
- Take someone some freshly baked cookies or homemade soup.
- Take someone store-bought cookies or store-bought soup from the deli.
- Send a "thinking of you" card.
- Give the gift of listening to an older person talk about "the olden days".
- Get in the habit of turning off your cell phone when in conversation.
- Offer to do heavier housework or seasonal chores around the house.
- Take someone who no longer drives to the drugstore or grocery store.
- Remember a shut-in on their birthday; go out for an ice cream cone.
- Sit and color together in adult coloring books – furnish the supplies.
- Take someone to shop at the Goodwill or a resale shop.
- Give a lonely person a hug. Hold their hand.
- Thank a veteran for serving our country; listen if they want to talk about it.
- Pay for a haircut for a patient in a nursing home.
- Give an elderly person a new sweater as they are often cold.
- Offer to help pay bills or offer budgetary assistance.
- Call and arrange to take a lonely person to lunch.
- Provide transportation to medical appointments.
- Play cards and board games.
- Make dates to read a book to a resident in an assisted living home.
- Take an older person for a ride to see the countryside.
- Work a jigsaw puzzle together while you chat.

The whole idea of volunteering your time is to bring an unexpected moment of joy to someone who needs to be reminded that they are not forgotten. A compassionate world can begin with one simple act of kindness.

Epilogue
## UNEXPECTED BLESSINGS

One day I was waiting to be checked out at Walmart when the man in the line next to me looked over, smiled, and asked, "Are you the Singing Lady?"

A little surprised as I stood there in my winter coat instead of my Hospice jacket, I had no idea who he was, but answered, "Yes, I am. And how are you doing this morning?"

He leaned against his cart and replied with a heavy sigh, "Not too good. It was one month ago today that you walked into my wife's room and then you went to the side of her bed and sang, "Be Still My Soul" to her. I knew her soul was still because she was so peaceful. But my soul and my heart were breaking. She died about an hour after you left."

I took a couple of steps over to him and gave him a hug. As I turned to push my cart up to be checked out, the man who was standing right behind me said, "Hey, lady, could I have one of those hugs, too? My Rosie died last August."

So I hugged him, too. Realizing that I was holding up the line, I saw the impatient look of the teenage cashier with the purple hair. I apologized to her, but as I stood there in the silence watching her repetitive motions as she quickly moved my items along the belt, I heard the most amazing short conversation . . .

The man behind me said to the man in the aisle next to me, "Hey, Buddy, if you aren't in a hurry, would you like to go have a cup of coffee?" As I was putting my bags in my cart, I heard the answer......

"Oh, yes. I don't seem to have enough to do these days and I just came in here this morning hoping to find someone to talk to."

Once outside, as I was putting my sacks in the trunk of my car, I realized a couple of tears had fallen down my cheeks. How blessed I was to be in the right place at the right time twice. Once to just happen to walk in to a room in the Hospice Center as Jesus was leading the wife of a man I had never seen before into Heaven. And then to see our Lord lead that same man to meet and befriend another lonely man in a most unexpected place.

The Bible is full of the stories of miracles from long, long ago. They are still happening today.

# FINAL THOUGHTS

It has been impossible to write this book on the blessings of volunteering without being profoundly affected by the memories of certain experiences all over again.

In the sharing of these stories in this book, I have discovered the truth found in Proverbs 13:19, "…..a longing fulfilled is sweet to the soul."

It is with my deepest gratitude that I thank the people in this book who have inspired me with their courage and their love. I thank them for allowing this ordinary woman to "hold their hand" in the sharing of the wonders of her own extraordinary journey.

-- JB

Made in the USA
Columbia, SC
30 October 2017